The Headcovering

The Biblical Case for the Woman's Headcovering

A Short Series of Sermons, Notes, Commentaries, and Quotes on what the Bible has to say about The Headcovering.

by

Michael Bunker

The Headcovering

© Copyright 2013 by Michael Bunker.

ISBN 978-1481947015

FIRST PRINTING

All rights reserved. No portion of this book may be reproduced in any form, except for brief quotations in reviews, without the written permission of the author.

All quoted verses are from the authorized King James Bible.

For free articles, sermons, and downloadable audios:

www.michaelbunker.com

To contact Michael Bunker, please write to:

M. Bunker
1251 CR 132
Santa Anna, Texas 76878

The Headcovering

The Biblical Case for the Woman's Headcovering

by

Michael Bunker

Acknowledgments

To Danielle and my girls

Thank you to Stewart and David for all of your work in bringing this tract to print.

A sincere "thank you" to all of you who continue to support the work.

Table of Contents

Introduction 1

Headcoverings, or The Veil, Part 1 7

Headcoverings, or The Veil, Part 2 27

A Note 51

Appendix I: Art and Quotes from the Ancients 53

Appendix II: Christian Headcovering Quotes and Commentaries 73

How You Can Help 113

Other Books by Michael Bunker 123

Introduction

The first portion of this book consists of a short series of sermons I produced for our home Church community back in 2008. At the time, my voluminous theological library was packed away in boxes, and the neo-headcovering "movement" had not yet taken place. Finding information and biblical teaching on the woman's headcovering at that time was very difficult. Since these sermons were first published, there has been a great resurgence in interest in the covering, and I have received thousands of communications from people who have questions about this topic. Hardly a month goes by when I am not contacted by someone asking me to provide more info, or more research, on the woman's headcovering.

What I have done in this short booklet is gather together what materials I could find so that any interested truth-seeker might be able to receive a sufficient education on the historical and biblical understanding of the veil or headcovering, as well as access to the quotes and the opinions of earlier teachers in earlier epochs of Christendom. I hope this work will also serve as a good general overview of the most accepted Christian commentaries, etc. In general, this is a safe pattern to follow in studying any topic: First, we ask, what does the

Word of God say about it? Second, if there is some confusion, or contrary teaching out there about what the Bible means to say, or if it seems evident that modern teachers have veered widely from what were the accepted norms for the entire age of the Church, what has the Church had to say about it in the past? What did the Puritans and Reformers have to say? Can we learn anything on the topic from history, or from art?

From a deep and penetrating study of the issue, hopefully we will find wisdom. As the scripture saith, *"In the multitude of counsel there is safety."* (Prov. 11:14)

In dealing with professing christians in modern christianity today, there are multitudes of difficulties. We live in a tremendously dark time, theologically and spiritually. Historical and biblical ignorance abound; false teachers and worldling guides have invaded the "church" and increased its syncretism with the world. Any teaching today that smacks of "old school" or "strict" or worse... (shiver) "Old Testament," is immediately dismissed as cultish quackery, or legalistic manipulation. In most cases, people aren't even willing to look at any teaching or opinion that doesn't already accord with their own. I have actually had people say to me on many different occasions, and in many places all over the world, "I don't care what the Bible has to say about it. I know what I believe, and you can believe whatever you want to believe!" As if I believe things because I want to!

When I was writing the booklet about what the Bible had to say about THE BEARD, I ran into the greatest single objection of the modern day christian... They will say, "That was in the Old Testament, and therefore it doesn't apply today," or, "That was the LAW, I am under Grace!" On the topic of the woman's headcovering, you would think we would be clear of any real objections to the Christian woman covering her head, since the Bible, even in the New Testament, teaches plainly that the woman ought so to do. But herein we run into the other great objections that abound in modern "christianity":

1. "I know it says that, but it doesn't mean that TO ME."

2. "I know it says that, but elsewhere it says this..." (the contradicting scripture theory)

3. "My Pastor said that no matter what the bulk of 1 Corinthians 11 teaches, since Paul said that the hair was given for a covering, then that is what I am going to believe."

So in one case (the beard) our road is difficult because the Old Testament is clear on the subject, but the New Testament doesn't very specifically address the issue; and in this case (the woman's headcovering), our road is difficult because the New Testament DOES specifically address the case. Most modern christians though are not interested in what God thinks about the issue. If they can find something... anything... that will let them do what they already want to do anyway, then they will follow their hearts and not God's Word. After all, that is what they've been taught their whole lives... Follow Your Heart.

"The heart is deceitful above all things, and desperately wicked: who can know it?" (Jer 17:9)

It is true that the headcovering does not eradicate vanity. No obedience, however sincere, will solve all of the problems of sin and the heart.

Antisthenes was a Stoic philosopher who learned at the feet of Socrates. Being a Stoic, Antisthenes believed in simplicity and humility and even poverty. He was known for wearing a thread-bare cloak full of holes, and on one occasion, as he passed by Socrates, the great teacher said to him, *"Antisthenes, I can still see your vanity through the holes in your cloak."*

We cannot hide dark hearts with beards and headcoverings. Nor are these things always evidence of holiness, purity, obedience, chastity, or humility. To think that there is an external and carnal work that can accomplish spiritual things is to miss the point. We are to be obedient to the true and faithful teaching of God's Word *because* it is God's Word and therefore it is the exposition of His glorious mind on the topic. We are to be obedient because obedience is due to God. We are to be obedient, because the carnal things will not, themselves, do a work on or in us, but God often uses obedience to do His vital work in and through us. It is a false and diabolical argument to say that disobedience is better than obedience because obedience will engender vanity.

My purpose in compiling this book is so that honest and true seekers can see the arguments, quotes, scriptures, and teachings all in one place (as much as I've been able to gather).

I do ask you to read through the detailed commentaries and quotes in the Appendices of this book. It is there, as well as in the scriptures, that you will find opinions that are greater than mine.

Headcoverings, or The Veil, Part 1

"Were they ashamed when they had committed abomination? nay, they were not at all ashamed, neither could they blush: therefore they shall fall among them that fall: at the time that I visit them they shall be cast down, saith the LORD. Thus saith the LORD, Stand ye in the ways, and see, and ask for the old paths, where is the good way, and walk therein, and ye shall find rest for your souls. But they said, We will not walk therein. Also I set watchmen over you, saying, Hearken to the sound of the trumpet. But they said, We will not hearken" (Jer 6:15-17).

Let me preface this sermon by making an observation – one that will likely offend a good portion of the intended audience right from the outset – but one that needs to be made. There is a principle involved in the topic, and exposed in the primary biblical text covering the topic of the headcovering or veil, that needs to be understood. There is no single biblical topic, taken directly from the plain teaching of scripture, which is more likely to pierce "even to the dividing asunder of soul and spirit, and of the joints and marrow," and to discern "the thoughts and intents of the heart" (Heb. 4:12). According to the Scripture, the headcovering is patently designed and commanded by God to be a sign to show forth God's divine order – that between the man and the woman, and to typically represent the submission of man to God. So, by its very nature, you can imagine that this topic will be one that is highly hated and rejected by those who are in rebellion to God's divine order. It is a fact that the truth brought to light by a proper understanding of this topic will be received in direct relation to ones submission to God's divine order, and to God Himself.

Some of you may be surprised to see me start this discussion about headcoverings for women with this verse from Jeremiah. Surely (some will say) Jeremiah was not talking about women running about with their heads uncovered when he wrote these verses. I agree that he definitely was not - because he would have never imagined such a thing. It would have never crossed his mind that a society or culture claiming to follow and obey the God of Abraham, Isaac, and Jacob would permit such a blatant flaunting of God's divine order. I am also certain that Jeremiah was not thinking of homosexual acts committed by "ministers" when he penned these words. He could not have been thinking of child-molesting and man-buggering Catholic priests or of sodomite Protestant televangelists when he wrote this. I would doubt that any thought of the professing people of God allowing and even encouraging and defending blatant homosexuality ever crossed his mind. In fact, I would even go so far as to state that even those false prophets and wicked priests about whom — Jeremiah does speak — those who "committed abomination" and "were not ashamed," those who were bold to commit the most heinous of idolatries and who refused to hear the teaching of God's true watchmen; I do not believe even those false prophets and apostates would have suffered a homosexual preacher to live openly in the camp. I am certain that Jeremiah was not thinking of modern professing "christianity" when he penned these threats. I am sure he had no thought of half-baked "praise teams" where the women dress like harlots and the men dress like women. I am sure he had no inkling of Christmas pageants, Charismatic barking and laughter movements, Crystal Cathedrals, Starbucks and McDonalds franchises in church lobbies, man and wife "pastor" teams, exposed bellies and cleavage in the congregations, sky-high divorce rates, and every other type of foolish abominations out there masquerading as the true religion of the Holy God. No, in these verses Jeremiah was condemning Israel because of her covetousness, and because the people dealt falsely (Jer. 6:13), and because they were too involved in trade and commerce with the world (Jer. 6:20). They were indeed grievous revolters, slanderers, and corrupters, but I don't think even they would have imagined the horror that professes to be the religion of the One True

God today. But, I hardly think that we should throw out this verse as inapplicable, merely because the sins of the professing people of God today are a thousand times worse than those addressed in this verse by Jeremiah. Jeremiah's advice is sound, and it should apply to every area of our lives. If we are advised to stand in the paths, and to ask for the old paths wherein is the good way that we might walk therein, then it is our duty to study and seek out those paths.

I wanted to start out this series talking about the old paths, because there are too many lazy, modernist preachers out there who claim to be telling the people the truth, while they themselves are dealing falsely with God's people. Too many ministers, unlearned neophytes, and old, proud corrupters, are doing a terrible disservice to God's people by not telling them the whole truth. My purpose in this series is to show the old paths that we might walk in them; but in order to get to my argument, I will try to first examine why modern preachers and teachers are too afraid to preach what the Word of God actually says.

Modernist preachers and apostate apologists love to befuddle audiences with ill studied opinions on historical cultural practices, and literary citations violently wrenched from their context, and with these they seek to prove that modern innovations are actually acceptable and approved of God, even if they fly in the face of the plain text of scripture. The preacher is engaged in this act of scripture-wrenching for only one real purpose – to satisfy and satiate the lusts of his audience. Why do you think anyone would go to such lengths to prove that a direct command of God is no longer applicable, unless it is to gain some other benefit other than the acceptance and approbation of God? Every modern preacher knows (whether he will admit it or not) that if he preaches an unpopular truth, especially to women, that he will lose the approval of the worldly woman, and most likely he will lose the man as well – since in our day the man (both married and unmarried) is led around by the woman. No preacher wants to lose his audience, so his internal lust for approval and acceptance, and his weakness in the face of inevitable dissent, causes him to bend to the will of human corruption, rather than to the will of God Almighty.

Now I want to lay out a scenario for you, because I need to provide some depth of understanding to you so that you can understand why hard truths are no longer taught in the Church, and I need to do it before I can even get to the arguments I have in favor of the woman's veiling.

In our scenario, I (as the father of my children) have gone on a long journey, and I have left very specific ordinances and practices for my family to keep in my absence. Some of those ordinances are specific to the time when I will be gone, some are accepted automatically from long use – in that they are things that I have always required - and some are overriding principles that ought to guide my family in their decision making. One of the long-time laws of my family is that my family is always to dress modestly, and in no circumstance are they to go around without proper clothes on. This has been the accepted practice of my family for our whole lives together, and they understand this law completely. Now, in our fictional scenario, during my absence, a stranger – a playmate, comes to visit my children and takes them to the pond to go swimming. He convinces them that they can take their clothes off and go naked just while they are swimming. His argument is that it is a silly practice to swim while clothed, and it is ridiculous to restrict nakedness while someone is mostly covered up in the water, so why not swim naked? Many of the other families in the area enjoy skinny dipping, so it cannot be all bad. They are convinced by his arguments, and a few of them strip down and go skinny dipping in the pond. The others, those who refuse to be swayed by modernist arguments, are adamant that this new practice is unacceptable and is contrary to the rules and the law given by the father, and they protest and dispute with the offenders. Later, I come home and I find out what has taken place. I find out that the children have been hoodwinked and bamboozled by a stranger, so I carefully reiterate and strengthen the law to my children. I sit them down and I say:

"I am glad and I praise you that, until now, you have obeyed me and that you have kept the ordinances and rules that I gave to you. But I would have you know that God has placed me over you, and that you are not to follow the whims of strangers. Every one who goes swimming naked, dishonors me and dishonors God. If you will not be clothed while swimming because you think it is best not to be covered, then you should strip off your skin as well, maybe that will show you how shameful it is for you to go without clothing. But if you will not strip off your skin, then also do not strip off your clothing."

My argument is that, just as you would not go naked anywhere else, because you know that you ought not to and that it would make you a gazingstock and that it would dishonor your father you should not go naked while swimming just because someone told you it is alright. Just as it would be foolish and ridiculous to strip your skin off just because someone told you too, in the same way you should not strip off your clothes because someone told you it is acceptable.

Note that the acceptable practice for the children at the time was that we are to be clothed in public at all times. I am dealing with a particular infraction, and I am extending the overall law to cover the exception that was created by deceivers. I am not making a cultural argument that is applicable only to this one generation, nor am I creating a local ordinance that is applicable only in my own pond.

Now, imagine that much time has passed. My rules still exist and have been written down in writing for future generations of my family. Several generations later, some of my great-grandchildren have a strong desire to go skinny-dipping, and they chafe against the long held traditions and laws against it. They make the argument that my law is no longer in effect, because nakedness has become more popular since then, and, after all, I was only writing to my own immediate children and only in that particular time. But alas, no one falls for it at first, and the new innovation is disallowed. The parents remember the practice of their own parents, so the rule stays in effect for another generation or two.

Then one day, the children of a new generation, while reading my exhortations, find a loophole in the argument. They say, "He was only speaking of not being naked 'WHILE SWIMMING'. It plainly says here, "everyone who goes swimming naked," it doesn't say that we have to be clothed all of the rest of the time. So as long as we are covered when we swim, then we are alright! Soon, all the children are walking around naked. The older folks are offended, and they protest and write treatises against public nakedness, but they are laughed to scorn. The children stay naked all of the time, but only put on clothes to go swimming – as per their new understanding of my original command.

Now, when these corrupt children grow up to be parents themselves, having lived a lifetime going around naked in public, they find it ridiculous and hypocritical to require their own children to wear clothing while they swim. They resort back to the original argument, that the command of the Patriarch was only to apply to his own children in that generation. It should not apply to anyone else. So, soon the commandment is forgotten and abandoned altogether. It is looked upon as a cultural relic, and an antiquated practice maybe good for its time, but useless in a new and modern world.

So, how would you like to be the preacher or the parent, generations later, who has to say - Whoa! We not only should not be swimming naked, but we ought to be fully and modestly clothed all the time! How popular do you think you will be? Can you anticipate the attacks and the slanders? Can you predict the arguments that will be made to maintain the abominable, but accepted, status quo? I think you can if you try hard enough. It should be understood that no preacher today is expected to comment or examine the following scriptures at all, unless it is with the view of explaining the plain text away, and of relegating it to a museum of antiquated cultural anomalies of the past, something not relevant to Christ's Church today:

"Every man praying or prophesying, having his head covered, dishonoureth his head. But every woman that prayeth or prophesieth with her head uncovered dishonoureth her head: for that is even all one as if she were shaven. For if the woman be not covered, let her also be shorn: but if it be a shame for a woman to be shorn or shaven, let her be covered" (1Co 11:4-6).

Imagine for a minute that you are a sincere and diligent Christian, a member of the Body of Christ in any nation, and in any time past (most any time prior to the 20th Century, and absolutely any time prior to the 19th Century). Study for yourself and find out if a woman would have been permitted to go around with her head uncovered in that century. Those of you who are old enough will know the answer already. Even in America, one of the most religiously liberal countries in the world, up until very recently a woman was expected to be wearing a headcovering during the public fellowship and assembly. Even when I was a child, women had "Sunday Chuch bonnets" and were expected to wear them. Now, I confess that by that time, the women had already abandoned the practice of covering themselves at all times, because that practice had disappeared a few generations earlier; but even as recently as 40-50 years ago, women went to Church services with their heads covered. I have a picture of the Roman Catholic president John F. Kennedy and his wife Jackie going to Church in the early 1960's, and she is wearing a headcovering. But imagine that you are a diligent and sincere Christian living in the 1700's, or the 1400's, or pick any other century all the way back to the time of Christ. Do you believe that a woman went around with their head uncovered? Of course they didn't, and I'll prove that in the next part, but any legitimate and honest study of history and literature proves the point. But I have heard the most outrageous and ridiculous arguments from people (mainly men) trying to prove that many women in the first few centuries (and even those in the Corinthian Church) went around all day with their heads uncovered. This assertion is ridiculous and is unsupported by any historical documents taken in context. So, in our scenario, we can see that it was never the practice of the professing Church of Jesus Christ on this earth, until very recently, for a woman to go around uncovered. It wasn't until the late 1900's and early on in the 20th Century that the innovation became the general practice. Now, most of the historical arguments against the woman's headcovering have followed the pattern of my initial fictional story. First, the headcovering was abandoned outside the Church, but it was maintained in the public worship, because even the false preachers and false prophets of the day could not then get away from Paul's plain teaching here in 1ˢᵗ Corinthians. Then, much later, even in our own day and in the time of our parents, the headcovering was abandoned inside the fellowship and the assembly of worshipers. This was accomplished primarily by the argument that God's commandment through Paul no longer applies in our own culture and time, but that it was written specifically and only to the Corinthians and only for that particular generation. I will address all of the arguments against the headcovering in detail throughout the lesson, but I would remind the fair and honest hearer that the modern practice of the woman going uncovered is a new innovation, not supported in Scripture, and not the practice of the true Church in any age.

So, before I deal with the specific arguments that are often made in defense of the new innovations, let me make a plain statement of our position concerning what the historical record says, and, in relation to that, what was the practice of the Church of all times concerning the woman's headcovering.

1. It was the practice of the Church to obey the ordinances given to them by Paul and the Apostles, especially concerning the fellowship of the beloved. These were not "church specific," "culture specific," or "era specific"

ordinances, but were the practices of the Church as practiced from the very beginning, even during the time of Christ, and they were passed by Apostolic authority to the Church in Corinth by the authority of Christ vested in His selected vessel – the Apostle Paul. (1 Cor. 11:2), and were then codified in Holy Scripture, which is our rule of faith, life, and practice.

2. Paul has shown forth his own practice, in this very book, of specifically stating when the ordinance or practice that he is suggesting or commanding, is NOT the command of the Lord Jesus Christ. In 1 Cor. 7:25, concerning the idea of abstinence or celibacy among men, Paul states that in this case he is giving his own mind on the subject and not the law as commanded by Jesus Christ. This, then, ought to be a precedent that shows us that Paul is willing to let us know when he is giving the ordinance of Christ, and when he is giving the opinion of Himself.

3. Prior to the necessity of this letter, it was the practice of the Hebrews, and then the Jewish Church, and then the Gentile Church in all areas, for the woman to have her head covered (or veiled) in public at all times. The anomaly he is addressing, that of women uncovering themselves in public worship, was a new

innovation at the time, and it was causing a disturbance and distress in the Church.

4. Paul does not make his argument in order to enforce a Jewish practice on Greeks and Romans, or to enforce a Greek practice on Jews and Romans. It was evidently, according to Plutarch, the practice of Roman women to go around with their heads covered, but Paul was not likely to be imposing a Roman practice on Jews and Greeks. Paul, instead, is mandating the custom as it was given to Him by Christ, regardless of its application to any particular culture. The argument can be unequivocally made that it was the general practice (with a few exceptions among Greek women) in all three cultures for the woman to have her head covered in some manner any time she was in public, but Paul makes no statement validating the customs or style of one culture over another; rather, he insists that the new practice, that of the woman uncovering herself specifically for public worship, is un-godly, unacceptable, inconsistent with God's divine order, and dishonorable.

5. There were, however, some overriding principles and realities which would have guided Paul, over and above his desire to give to the Church of Jesus Christ a pure form of public worship as commanded by Christ. Paul

was a Jew, and in no place did Paul overthrow or overturn the law (except where Christ had already done so) for cultural relevancy or political expediency. God Himself said, "After the doings of the land of Egypt, wherein ye dwelt, shall ye not do: and after the doings of the land of Canaan, whither I bring you, shall ye not do: neither shall ye walk in their ordinances. Ye shall do my judgments, and keep mine ordinances, to walk therein: I am the LORD your God" (Lev 18:3-4). God also had forbidden the Jews to clothe themselves in foreign attire: "And it shall come to pass in the day of the LORD'S sacrifice, that I will punish the princes, and the king's children, and all such as are clothed with strange apparel" (Zep 1:8). So it is not only unlikely, but impossible that Paul was, on his own whim and due to cultural or political pressures, satiating the desires of the people of God to throw off their own practices and to conform themselves with the culture or age where they found themselves.

6. The practice of the woman uncovering herself during worship was adopted by many, because of the prevailing strength of the pagan mystery cults in Corinth. Remember that Christianity was a very new thing at this time, and it would not be strange to see women, particularly of the Roman and Greek sects, bringing in the practices of their former religion to the worship

of the one true God. Note, too, that Paul specifically mentions that it was while praying and prophesying that these women were in the practice of uncovering themselves. This is understandable because in many of the Pagan Mystery cults, the women – following the practice of men in the mainstream religions – had adopted the practice of unveiling themselves before praying or prophesying.

7. Neither in the original Greek, nor in the English, does Paul support his command by appeals to political exigency or cultural relevancy, but in fact he prefaces his argument by commending the Corinthian Church for obeying the ordinances and practices of the Church specifically as they were given by Paul, without regard to their own personal opinions or cultural expectations on the subject.

8. Paul's argument was not designed to address any issue other than that which is in view, namely, the wearing of headcoverings in public worship – and specifically while a woman is praying or prophesying. His statement was NOT a rejection or abdication of the already accepted social, cultural, and religious laws restricting a woman from being uncovered outside of the public worship. This was not an invitation for the woman to go uncovered

elsewhere, because it didn't address that practice at all – since that practice would have been unheard of, and would have been considered an abomination and shameful at the time, particularly to anyone from a Jewish background. Nor was Paul giving women permission to uncover themselves at all times other than when they are praying and prophesying – that would be an unacceptable and unseemly twisting of his words and intentions. It is like if I told my son, "Don't hit your sister because you are mad at her," it would be silly to say that it is acceptable to hit your sister any other time, just so long as you aren't mad at her.

9. Paul did not make a complete and logical legal argument in order to erase its impact by later claiming that the woman's hair was sufficient for a covering. We will address that argument sufficiently in the second part of this book.

There is another point that I want to make before I conclude this first part, and rest assured we will be handling all the objections to Paul's ordinance in the next part of the series, but I began this exercise by pointing out that most people, specifically the preachers, will not want to hear, and certainly will not obey, the commandment concerning women's headcoverings. They will not hearken to the Word of God, because their internal corruptions will not allow them to hear the truth:

> *"Thus saith the LORD, Stand ye in the ways, and see, and ask for the old paths, where is the good way, and walk therein, and ye shall find rest for your souls. <u>But they said, We will not walk therein</u>"* (Jer 6:16).

Note the principle. God's children are not to stand in the new ways and ask for new paths, but they are to ask for the old paths and stand in the old ways. Israel was a type of the Church, and God forbade Israel from being absorbed into the culture and from adopting the practices of the people 'round about them. Matthew Henry said,

"The Jews being a peculiar people, they were thus distinguished from their neighbours in their dress, as well as in their diet, and taught by such little instances of singularity not to be conformed to the way of the heathen in greater things. Thus likewise they proclaimed themselves Jews wherever they were, as those that were not ashamed of God and his law."

The Israelites were consistently commanded to not take on the ways of the people, and they were commanded to dress in a way that was particular and peculiar to themselves, and to never allow themselves or their culture to be changed or assimilated because of political or cultural expediency. Today's preacher places cultural relevancy as the hallmark of his argument to the Church. He cannot preach hard things, so he preaches soft ones. His flock says, "Prophesy not unto us right things, speak unto us smooth things, prophesy deceits" (Isaiah 30:10). His job is as a masseuse of strained consciences and as a false physician to a plagued people. He will never exhort his people to look to the old paths, because if they dare to look there, they will learn that he has lied to them and misled them, and that he has served himself rather than God. The great commentator John Gill likens the command to ask for the old paths and to stand in the old ways to a man who must backtrack down the path to find a signpost that will once again put him back in the right way. Well, if Christians were to actually do that, they will find that it is the preacher who has led them astray, and then where will he be? So instead of good counsel, he gives them new doctrines and cultural innovations, all to keep them adhered to him. It is a sad thing, but this is a fact. Only a diligent searcher, one who is willing to obey the direct command of God – that he be willing to ask for the old paths, and stand in the old ways, wherein is the good way – will find rest for his soul. The bulk of men and women will say, "We will not walk therein," and "we will not hearken." Therefore, it is said, that "they shall fall among them that fall" - and that is the sad reality that neither the modern teacher, nor the modern student, desires to face.

If the Lord wills, we will look deeper into this topic in the next part.

Headcoverings, or The Veil, Part 2

Every man praying or prophesying, having his head covered, dishonoureth his head. But every woman that prayeth or prophesieth with her head uncovered dishonoureth her head: for that is even all one as if she were shaven. For if the woman be not covered, let her also be shorn: but if it be a shame for a woman to be shorn or shaven, let her be covered. For a man indeed ought not to cover his head, forasmuch as he is the image and glory of God: but the woman is the glory of the man. For the man is not of the woman; but the woman of the man. Neither was the man created for the woman; but the woman for the man. For this cause ought the woman to have power on her head because of the angels. (1Co 11:4-10)

We have shown in the previous part that it was the almost universal practice of women of every culture represented in Corinth when this epistle was written to cover their heads in some manner. And we have made a point of showing that Paul's intent was NOT that women would cover themselves during prayer or worship – as if it were acceptable (or even a common practice) for them to go uncovered at other times. Neither the context, nor a thorough review of the history, society, and culture allows that interpretation (though I have heard it many, many times from modernist preachers). Rather, Paul was making the point that a woman ought not to uncover herself during prayer and public worship, as was being done by some who had adopted that practice from the pagans. This point, I believe, is where the greatest misunderstandings and deceptions occur in relation to this verse. Please make note of that, and pray about it in your own study of the issue. Out of ignorance of the context, the writing style, and the prevailing culture, many have come to the conclusion that Paul was making a sociological argument – or a cultural one, even though in his introduction to this chapter, Paul places this discourse in the arena of absolute ordinances that he expects the people to obey and keep. Further, he raises the bar even higher by making the argument that a woman ought to have "power" (or the veil, or covering) on her head "because of the angels." We will discuss more about what this statement means particularly in the proper place, but we need to note that Paul nowhere appeals to the culture or to the practice of the surrounding peoples. Had he done so, the liberals (on this issue) would still fail in proving their point, since it is evident by a thorough study of the time that the Greek women, the Roman women, and the Hebrew women all (with very few exceptions) wore headcoverings, and, as we showed in the first part, this convention was practiced by all biblical cultures even into our very day. It has been abandoned quite recently, and we did discuss how this abandonment came about. Instead, however, Paul based his argument on universal truths, such as spiritual order, authority, and on nature – all things that are not changed, altered, abolished, or affected by time, place, practice, or culture. It would be quite a ridiculous argument for the liberal to state that at one point angels (either good or bad) might be affected by the woman being uncovered, but that now "Angel-culture" has developed to the point that a woman being uncovered no longer has the same effect. In any case, as we have said, Paul does not rest his argument on such silly and changeable ground. He builds his argument on a much more permanent foundation – that a woman ought to be veiled:

Because by wearing the veil she shows forth the proper relationship between Christ and man, man and woman, and Christ and the Church.

Because the woman is a type, and in order for the type to be properly portrayed, the woman ought to be covered.

Because the woman is created for the man, and the cover is a constant reminder to her, and to the society, of her proper position.

Because it is "uncomely," which in this context means "unsuitable, or improper," for a woman to pray to God uncovered.

Because just as God has given a woman long hair to distinguish her from a man, in the same way, she is to be distinguished in her submission by the covering of her head.

Because there is no tradition or custom in the Churches of God of the woman going uncovered, or being permitted to uncover herself during prayer or public worship.

Because a woman's veil is necessary on account of the angels.

So Paul makes his argument on many grounds, and nowhere claims that he is only giving his own opinion, or that local customs or generational practices ought to trump these very sound and transcendent arguments.

In this part, I intend to answer the most common objections to the woman's headcovering. We should note that the theological liberal is willing to stand on the flimsiest of arguments, and some of them make no appeal at all to the Scripture, or even to the arguments made in Scripture. Many arguments against the woman's veil are based completely and utterly on things outside of the Bible or anything God might have to say on the subject. The primary objections to the woman's headcovering are those that appeal only to "feelings," "emotions," or are those which have worldliness and syncretism as their root. A man called me on the phone many years ago (many years before the truth of this subject was made clearer to me). He was shocked because he had just returned home from a meeting where the women (GASP!) wore headcoverings! This man was nearly in tears. He said, "Michael... Oh, Michael! Those people have their women in BONDAGE!!!" I remember laughing at the time, because I could not imagine at all how a woman choosing to wear a headcovering in order to obey the Bible, honor God, and her husband was "bondage." I told the man that, although we (at that time) did not practice headcoverings for women, I sure believed it to be a sign of honor and reverence, and could not for a moment believe that it was bondage – any more than requiring a woman to wear modest clothing (or any clothing at all for that matter) would be bondage. For several years, I would always go back to that call in my mind when I was thinking about what had gone wrong in the professing "church." The so-called "church" had slipped so far from any semblance of biblical truth, that comfort and freedom had become idols, and libertinism had become synonymous with heroism. By that I mean that men like the man who had called me actually considered themselves to be heroic because they were "freeing" women to operate by their baser fallen instincts. A year or so ago I got into a discussion with a young man who had pointed out to his pastor that the women in the Church were dressing more and more like whores. He told the pastor that the women were dressing like they were going to a nightclub to pick up men, and not like they were going to spend a time of worship and fellowship with God's children. The young man told me that his pastor claimed that to restrict their free expression would be "bondage," and that he did not want to be so legalistic. You'll note that "legalism" has become a weapon that is to be used against obedience. It is considered a trump card that can be played any time someone makes an argument based on propriety, modesty, etc. All of Paul's arguments in support of the headcovering would be called "legalistic" if they were made today. I will list here a few more arguments that are along the same lines, or which are based on the same type of logic:

- The headcovering makes the woman a gazingstock, and a spectacle, and exposes her to ridicule.

- The headcovering makes the woman (and the group or church) look "cultish."

- The headcovering demeans the woman, and makes men think she is less than a person, and that she is not to be respected.

- The headcovering makes the woman "unattractive."

Now, you will notice that none of these arguments are based on the Bible. Most are not even based on morality or right and wrong. In fact, all four of these arguments are based on "psychology" and not on Christianity. All four are ridiculous, and are easily refuted, but we do want to point out their faulty basis first. Here are my quick refutations of these four arguments (and the principles in my refutations can be applied to any such psychological or sociological arguments):

- That a woman is made into a spectacle by wearing a headcovering. I would argue that a woman who dresses modestly, who behaves in accordance with Scripture, who honors her husband (or head), and who attempts to live godly in Christ Jesus, etc., will already be a gazingstock and a spectacle. I would further argue that all Christians (both men and women) who do so obey the scripture that they ignore the hatred of the world, will be a spectacle to those around them, and that this is to be expected, and is in fact prophesied to be the case: Yea, and all that will live godly in Christ Jesus shall suffer persecution (2 Tim. 3:12). But call to remembrance the former days, in which, after ye were illuminated, ye endured a great fight of afflictions; Partly, whilst ye were made a gazingstock both by reproaches and afflictions; and partly, whilst ye became companions of them that were so used. (Heb 10:32-33)

- That the practice of women wearing headcoverings makes the woman (and the group) "cultish." First, I would point out that what people mean when they say "cultish" is that the group or practice does not match up to worldly norms. In other words, since the practice makes a woman or group look "unworldly," that it should be considered "cultish." Now, the largest cult in the world is the cult of modernism, fad, and idolatry that we call "the culture," and it is evident that Christ called us to be different, to look different, and to act differently than the world culture. So here, again, we have just another argument for syncretism and worldliness. Whatever the world decides is "cultish" is to be avoided, and whatever the world decides is acceptable is to be embraced. Can you think of any argument in the entire world that is more unbiblical than that? I tell you that this is the reason that most women, even most professing Christian women, will not obey God in this area. It comes down to either this argument, that to wear a headcovering makes them look like they are in a cult, or it is the argument from vanity (which we will discuss more in a moment) that stops women from obeying God concerning the covering of the head.

- That the practice of wearing a headcovering demeans the woman. I can tell you that this is only true in the eyes of the world, and the worldling. Only a worldly God-hater would think that a modestly dressed woman, who is doing her best to obey God and honor her husband, is demeaned by doing so. Only someone so infected by the depravity that has come upon man from rebellion against a Holy and Righteous God could ever conceive of a woman being "lessened" or demeaned by covering herself. In fact, it is a commentary on society and on individuals, that they believe this to be the case. In a rational, reasonable, biblically sound culture, we would look at a woman who is emphasizing her body as demeaning herself. We would consider a woman who is selling sexuality in public, who is attempting to draw men to herself by means of that over which she has no control (her sexual attractiveness), and which least exhibits her truth and value, as demeaning herself. And contrariwise, we would look at a woman who attempted to go around modestly, and to emphasize her morality and her superior culture, as opposed to her baser and more fleeting charms, as being superior. What kind of society is it, and what kind of person is it, that could possibly conclude that a woman is being demeaned by being covered? It is plain that human depravity is responsible for such a notion.

- That a headcovering makes a woman unattractive. The subtle argument here is that men want to hide the beauty of women in order to mitigate or lessen their power. By making this argument, the claimant logically must believe that a woman's true value and her authority and claim on power is based on her ability to make men want to have sex with her. This, again, is a commentary on our corrupt and wicked society. Unhappily, it is true that most women today traffic in this kind of wickedness. When we use the word "attractive," we ought to know what that word signifies. To "attract" means to "draw by a physical force," or to "draw by means of the emotions, or by the senses." This, then, puts "attraction" in opposition to reason and the mind. When the worldling says a woman is "attractive," he means that she is able to draw others (and thereby utilize power) because of carnal things that are easily manipulated. She may use surgery, makeup, and other tactics (all forms of lies) to "attract," but in every case she is utilizing those things which are contrary or irrespective of the mind. So, if it is claimed that a man wants to keep a woman "unattractive" by having her wear a headcover, then we can say that the results of his actions would be both biblical and sensible. If it were true (and it is not in any case I know or have heard of) that a woman is prevented from manipulating and lying by use of the headcover, then it must be said that she is being done a great service by the requirement. However, we cannot agree at all that a woman is made less beautiful (if that is what is intended) by the headcovering. Since the Bible claims that a woman is the type of the true Church, and that the true Church exists for the purpose of glorifying Jesus Christ, then any woman who desires to properly fulfill the role for which she was created would wear a headcovering. And any person who is motivated by God's Spirit, knowing what glory God receives by such obedience, would find nothing at all more beautiful than such a simple expression of obedience to God's will. As we are transformed by God's power, and as we become more aligned with God's will and mind, we find our proclivities and desires changed. We find beautiful what the world rejects, and we find glorious what the world finds repellent. We must remember that the kingdom of this world has redefined (and continues to always redefine) what is "beauty." Christianity is not supposed to change with the times, or to define itself by the definitions of the world.

Ok, the next few objections, which we have already refuted quite handily (though we will quickly mention them again here) are those which are based on false cultural or sociological assumptions. We usually call these the "time" or "culture" arguments. They generally follow or are likened unto these:

- Paul was only speaking to the Corinthians. He was dealing with a particular situation in Corinth alone, and his commandment is in no way binding on anyone else.

- Paul was only speaking to the people of that time. He was teaching in a time when it was common for women to wear headcoverings; and since women no longer wear headcoverings, the commandment no longer applies.

- In addition to the above arguments, Paul was only speaking about "while praying or prophesying," so he only meant "in church."

Answers:

- Paul clearly was not only speaking to the Corinthians. He had every intention that the principles involved would apply to every Church in all time. Paul also, in this very book, makes a point of delineating between that which he speaks by way of commandment, and those times when he is giving his own opinion. Paul gives this commandment under the topic of "ordinances," which were given to the Churches, which Paul expected the Christians to obey. We also note that, as we mentioned in the first part, Paul makes his argument for headcoverings and AGAINST the pagan cultural practice of the woman uncovering during prayer and worship. And again, his arguments are made on transcendent and spiritual grounds, and not on temporal and cultural ones. We also note that the commandment was kept as the practice of the Church throughout the generations until our very own day. We also will offer a quote towards the end of this sermon, from Tertullian, which proves that even unto the 2nd Century, the Corinthian Church still required the veiling of all women.

- Paul was clearly not speaking only to the people of that time. It would be a frail and weak argument and ordinance indeed that relied on acceptable norms based on "time" in order to make a statement of propriety or "comeliness" (suitableness). This argument is identical to that made by small children: "Well, everyone else is doing it!" Can you imagine teaching your children that it is inappropriate to run around naked merely because it is unacceptable today? Would you tell your children that they can take off their clothes in public so long as everyone else is doing it? Does something wrong become right merely by the passing of time? If Paul makes an argument based on the condition and position of <u>angels</u>, is it safe or even logical to then state that his argument was a time-based one?

- Paul was not limiting the commandment to "prayer and prophesying." I do understand where people get this argument, and in fact I have used it myself, though I must now admit it was out of ignorance. Paul was not saying that woman ought to cover herself only in prayer and public worship. To make that argument one would have to assert that it was a common or acceptable practice for a woman at that time to go uncovered at other times in public. Well, history shows that it was not. It was not the practice of the Romans, the Hebrews, or the Greeks for their women to go around uncovered. We can discern, then, from the context of the argument, and from a study of the history and culture of the time, that Paul was dealing with a practice that had infected the Church from the paganistic practices of the time - particularly from the Diana cult, which was prominent in the area at the time. The practice Paul was rejecting was the practice of the woman uncovering herself during prayer and worship. So this is not an argument that it is acceptable for a woman to be uncovered when she is not in prayer and worship.

Now we proceed to that argument that seems to be the most prominent. It is said by some that Paul, after making numerous heavy arguments in favor of the veil and of the covering of the head, now reverses himself and eliminates all of his own arguments by claiming in verse 15 that a woman's hair is sufficient for a headcovering:

> *But if a woman have long hair, it is a glory to her: for her hair is given her for a covering.* (1Co 11:15)

So it is the practice of some (or most, we might say) to take this one verse as an "out" or an exception to all that has come before. This conclusion can only be reached by stripping this verse from its context and by the apparent meaning of the author. As we have shown, Paul has built a lock-solid case in the preceding 12 verses that God, nature, practice, and moral necessity all require a woman to cover her head. Here, then, the argument is made that Paul turns all of that context upside down, erasing any purpose or reason behind all of his previous comments, and that he now permits a woman to pray and prophesy uncovered. Remember that it was not the practice of any of the prevalent cultures in Corinth for the women to go around unveiled. Nor did it become the practice of those claiming to be the Churches of God for another 1900 years. If this verse was designed as permission for a woman to go around unveiled, it is a curiosity that almost no biblical culture took advantage of that permission until the 20th century. Why do paintings and drawings of social life for the next many centuries all portray the woman (in public) as covered? What kind of sense would it make to overturn all of the great arguments Paul makes, with this one refutation of them? In fact, if this verse is looked at in the context of the overall argument made by Paul, it makes complete sense, and it is not contradictory at all. Let's look at it:

Verse 4: Every man who prays or prophesies with his head covered dishonors his head, which is a type of Christ, who is his spiritual head.

Verse 5: But since a man is the head of the woman, a woman who uncovers her head to pray or prophesy, dishonors her head, which is her husband. This is as if she had her head shaved!

We should note here that it was a great scandal for a woman to have her head shaved, or even if her hair was short. Paul here introduces the parallelism that the hair is to the head in the natural what the cover is to the head in the spiritual.

Verse 6: For if a woman is not covered, it is the same as if she were shaven and bald – which is to say it would be just as scandalous and ignominious a thing for a woman to be uncovered as it is for her to be bald. If, however, as any reasonable or sensible person must conclude, that it is heinous and scandalous for a woman to be bald, then in like manner she ought to wear a headcovering.

Verse 7: For a man indeed ought NOT to wear a cover on his head, since he is the image and glory of God; but the woman is the glory and honor of the man, which means that she ought to have a cover on her head.

Verse 8: Because, you see, the man is not of the woman, but the woman is of the man - because the woman came out of Adam's side.

Verse 9: All of this shows that the woman was made for man, and this is represented by her submission to him.

Verse 10: For this cause, and along this line of logic, we see that a woman ought to be covered because of the angels. Angels attend the divine worship, and they see things that are ordained of God along with the antitype they represent. The good angels are offended by that which wrongly represents God, or when the types and antitypes are destroyed by the whim and wish of men. Likewise, if evil angels are meant, the woman ought to cover herself that she be not the cause of lust in the spiritual realms. And, if this is not the case with evil angels, then she ought not give them cause to accuse her or her God by her willingness to cause men to lust.

Verse 11: Now, that said, we should note that mankind in worship to God - or the Church in worship to God - is not complete without the man and the woman represented together. The two types are both necessary to properly show forth the glory and wisdom of God.

Verse 12: Just as the woman was taken out of the man, when the rib was separated from Adam, the man is taken from woman in his birth. We should know that all of these pictures are given us from God, who would have us do all things appropriately.

Verse 13: Now, you all judge for yourself. Is it appropriate and seemly that a woman would uncover her head before praying to God who created all these types and shadows to glorify Himself?

Verse 14: Does not even nature teach you that if a man has long hair it is a shameful thing to him? He looks womanish and ought to be ridiculed for it.

Verse 15: But if a woman has long hair, which is only natural and expected, it is a glory to her! Don't you see how nature is showing us the proper way? Her hair is given her to represent a covering. It is given that she won't be bald, which, as we have shown, would be a shameful thing for her. Just as nature covered her head so that she would not be bald, she ought to cover her head so that she properly represents God and honors His authority and order structure.

Verse 16: Now, if all of these arguments don't convince someone; if they still seem contentious after all these numerous truths and evidences; if they still want to argue and disagree with it, then they aren't worth arguing with. Tell them that we (the Church) have no such custom of a woman uncovering her head in prayer and worship, and therefore that alone will suffice to shut his mouth. We don't allow it, and if reason will not convince him, then our practice and ordinances ought to.

So, as you can see, Paul was not eradicating his own argument in verse 15. He was continuing the point that a woman ought to be covered at all times in public, and ought not to uncover herself in prayer and worship. Her hair is given as an instruction, to teach her that she is different than a man, and that just because a man uncovers himself in worship and prayer, a woman is not permitted to do so.

Now, after all of these arguments, Paul concedes that some men will remain contentious. All the proofs will not convince them. All of the evidence will not convert them. To these we are merely to say, "It is not the practice or an ordinance of the Church to allow a woman to pray or prophesy uncovered." They will be judged for their actions, but we ought not to let them defile the congregation or the society just because they are contentious about something that Paul considers to be reasonable and obvious. We know that the human mind is capable of rationalizing any behavior, and that the natural man can explain away any disobedience at all. We also know that no one who is not motivated and operated by the Spirit of God will want to obey Him if there are any social or cultural consequences. We confess that obedience to this command today is difficult in the flesh, because all of those things that are at variance with God – namely the world, the flesh, and the devil – do not accept godly or spiritual things. Ask yourself this: who is glorified by the uncovered woman, God or the Devil. Whose work is done by the modernist woman and her painted, plaited, curled, and blow-dried hair? Ask if God's kingdom is advanced by the uncovered woman, or is the cause of lust, concupiscence, pride, and disorder advanced? Does the world hate headcoverings, or does it hate obedience? Think on these things.

If the reader were to acquaint himself with the writings of the first and second century, he would find how appalled the early Christians would be that we are even entertaining the thought of women going around in public uncovered. Clement of Alexandria wrote exhaustively on the subject, and I will quote from Tertullian who wrote an entire book opposing the African practice of allowing young girls (virgins) to remain without headcoverings.

First, I will quote what Tertullian had to say about how the Corinthians themselves understood Paul. Remember that the practice of the African Christians was that the older women had to be veiled and covered, but they were somewhat

47

licentiously allowing the younger women (virgins) to be uncovered. He appeals to the 2nd Century Corinthian Church, who even then still required all women, even virgins, to remain veiled:

> *"So, too, did the Corinthians themselves understand him. In fact, at this day the Corinthians do veil their virgins (virgines suas Corinthii velant). What the apostles taught, their disciples approve."* ("On the Veiling of Virgins" chap. 8, page 33- taken from the Ante-Nicene Fathers, Volume 4).

So you see, the Corinthians certainly understood what Paul was teaching, and the Apostle's disciples continued with that teaching.

I want to close here by making a statement that Paul himself makes as he approaches the closing of this letter to the Corinthians. I believe that the prevailing idea that "modern is better" and that the Church ought to model whatever the culture is doing, comes from an abandonment of the commandments of God. Some will argue that Paul was just giving his opinion, or that he was only talking to the Corinthians. But here is what he had to say to the Corinthians in this very book:

> *"What? came the word of God out from you? or came it unto you only? If any man think himself to be a prophet, or spiritual, <u>let him acknowledge that the things that I write unto</u>*

you are the commandments of the Lord. But if any man be ignorant, let him be ignorant" (1Co 14:34-38).

I would mention that this forceful statement is made within the commandment that women ought to remain silent in the Churches... But that is a sermon for another day.

A Note

Any argument for or against the necessity of the woman's headcovering must be fully based on the true, historic, and contextual teaching of God's Word. Emotion and tradition and human rationalizations must be left out of it. We must truly and seriously desire to know what God thinks about it. There can be no denying that we live in a time of moral depravity and spiritual darkness. The human mind and corrupt heart can rationalize any behavior whatsoever, and we know that this is true. The hardest truths to embrace are those that cost us some of what we have invested into our carnal man. Spiritual sounding platitudes and circumstantial excuses abound, but, in all times, obedience is costly and hard. I was surprised to find that the wisdom of the ancients and the truly spiritual throughout the age of the Church have really been unified on this topic. What follows is a pretty intensive examination of what the true Church has believed through time.

Although there will always be exceptions, and although apostasy and antichrist were already rearing their ugly heads as early as the first century, God has preserved a golden thread of truth within His Church, so that the gates of hell cannot prevail against it. I invite you to read all of these materials closely. Some of these cannot be found online anywhere, and I only discovered them by careful perusal of every book and set that I possessed in my library. I pray that the work bears fruit, and that you do, indeed, get a glimpse of what God thinks through the voices of His Church through time.

Michael Bunker

Appendix I: Art and Quotes from the Ancients

***Author's note: while we never refer to or quote the so-called "church fathers" as moral or spiritual authorities other than as they agree with and support the plain teaching of the Scriptures, we have no problem quoting them in instances where their particular testimony might give us a cultural insight into the ways and thinking of churchmen in a particular age. ~ MB

> *But I would have you know, that the head of every man is Christ; and the head of the woman is the man; and the head of Christ is God. Every man praying or prophesying, having his head covered, dishonoureth his head. But every woman that prayeth or prophesieth with her head uncovered dishonoureth her head: for that is even all one as if she were shaven.* 1 Corinthians 11:3-5

The following photos are etchings and artwork found in the Catacombs of Rome. While possibly idolatrous, they provide evidence to how the early Christian women applied the apostles instructions regarding the head covering.

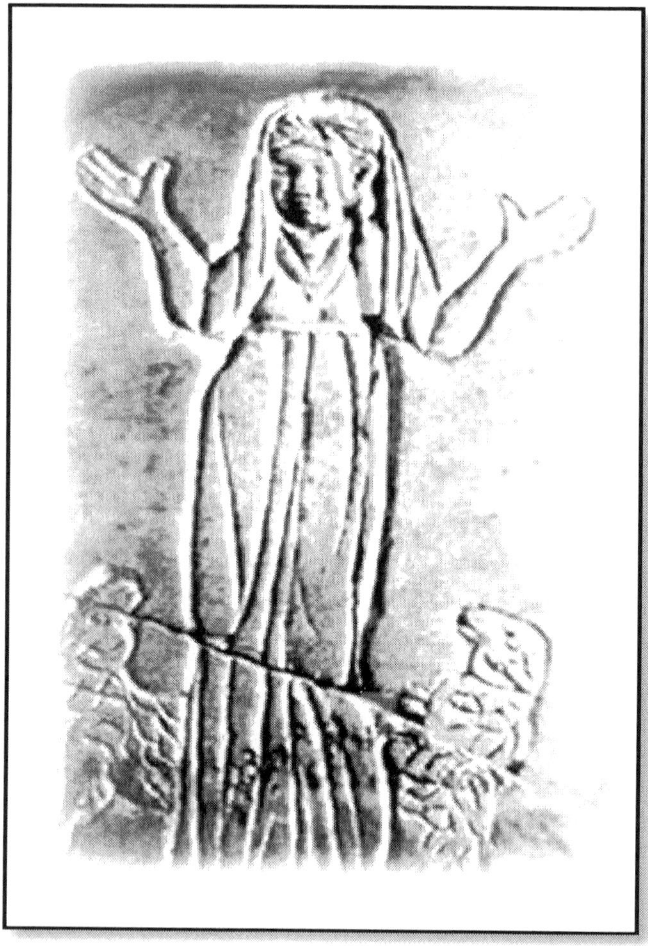

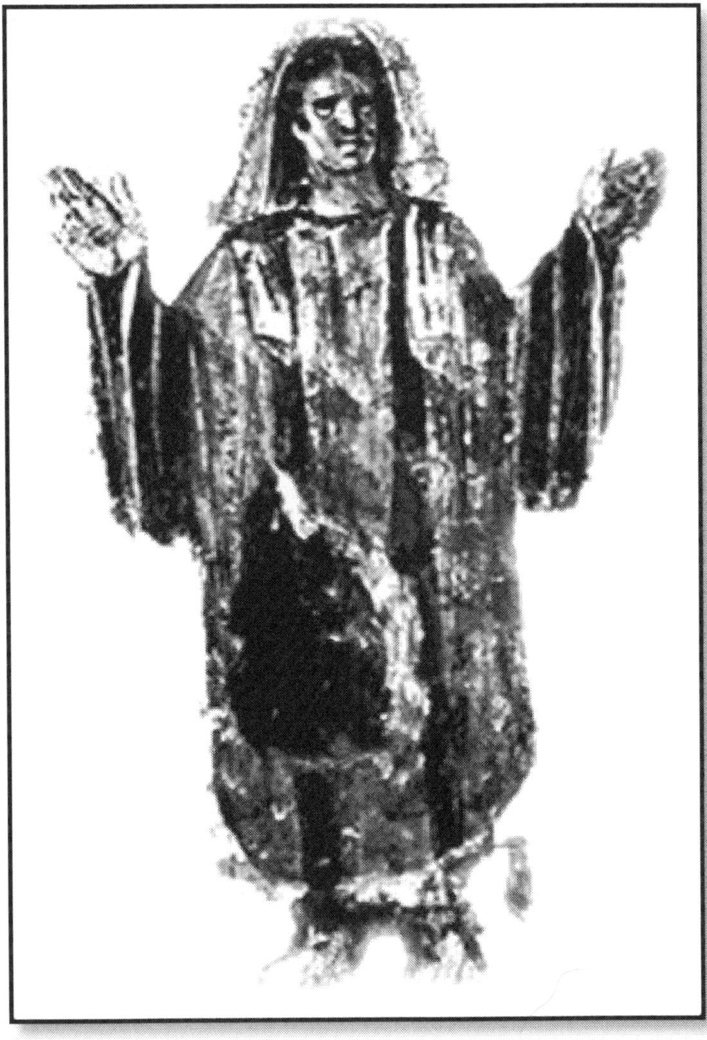

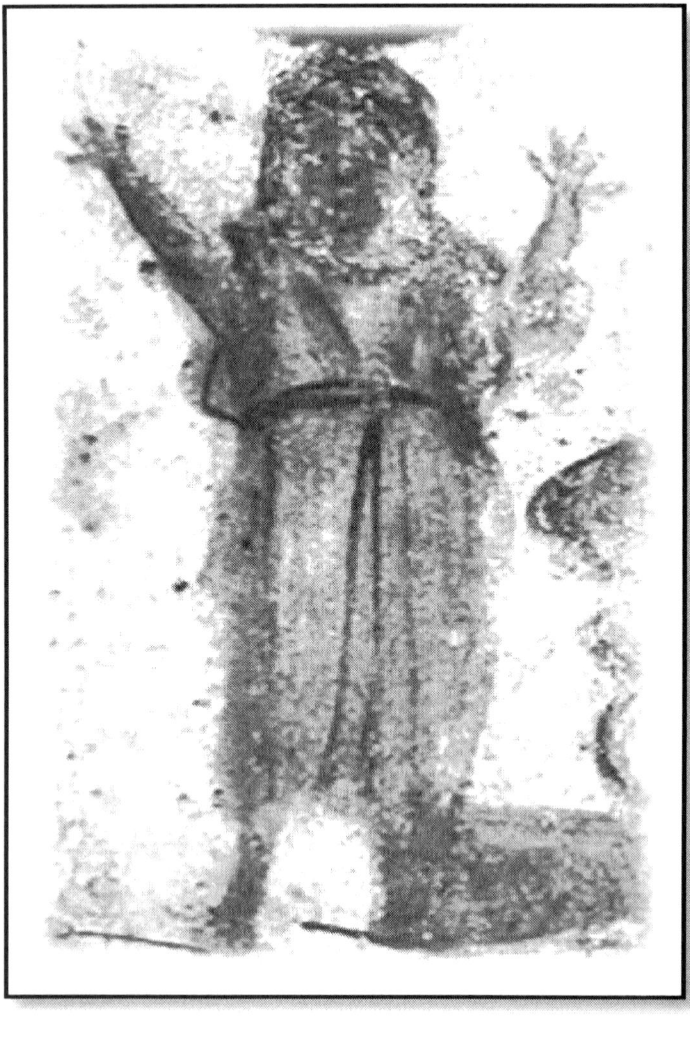

57

Quotes from some early Christians teachers about headcoverings:

HERMAS:

Now after I had passed the beast, and had gone forward about thirty feet, behold, there meets me a virgin arrayed as if she were going forth from a bridal-chamber all in white and with white sandals, veiled up to her forehead, and her head-covering consisted of a turban, and her hair was white. Hermas (A.D. 150) Ante-Nicene Fathers vol.1 pg. 18

CLEMENT OF ALEXANDRIA:

Although such a covering ought to be assumed as is requisite for covering the eyes of women. Clement of Alexandria (A.D. 195) Ante-Nicene Fathers vol.2 pg.265

It has also been commanded that the head should be veiled and the face covered; for it is a wicked thing for beauty to be a snare to men. Nor is it seemly for a woman to wish to make herself conspicuous, by using a purple veil. Clement of Alexandria (A.D. 195) Ante-Nicene Fathers vol.2 pg.266

And she will never fall, who puts before her eyes modesty, and her shawl; nor will she invite another to fall into sin by uncovering her face. For this is the wish of the Word, since it is becoming for her to pray veiled. Clement of Alexandria (A.D. 195) Ante-Nicene Fathers vol.2 pg.290

CHRYSOSTOM:

"Thou standest with angels; thou singest with them; thou hymnest with them; and yet dost thou stand laughing?" Bengel explains, "As the angels are in relation to God, so the woman is in relation to man. God's face is uncovered; angels in His presence are veiled (Isa 6:2). Man's face is uncovered; woman in his presence is to be veiled. For her not to be so, would, by its indecorousness, offend the angels (Mat 18:10, Mat 18:31). She, by her weakness, especially needs their ministry; she ought, therefore, to be the more careful not to offend them."

TERTULLIAN:

Demanding then a law of God, you have that common one prevailing all over the world, engraved on the natural tables to which the apostle too is wont to appeal, as when in respect of the woman's veil he says, "Does not even Nature teach you?" - as when to the

Romans, affirming that the heathen do by nature those things which the law requires, he suggests both natural law and a law-revealing nature. Tertullian (A.D. 198) Ante-Nicene Fathers vol.3 pg. 96

Christ is the Head of the Christian man - (for his head) is as free as even Christ is, under no obligation to wear a covering, not to say a crown. But even the head which is bound to have the veil, I mean woman's, as already taken possession of by this very thing, is not open also to a crown. She has the burden of her own humility to bear. Tertullian (A.D. 198) Ante-Nicene Fathers vol.3 pg. 102

But that point which is promiscuously observed throughout the churches, whether virgins ought to be veiled or no, must be treated of. For they who allow to virgins immunity from head-covering, appear to rest on this; that the apostle has not defined "virgins" by name, but "women," as "to be veiled;" Tertullian (A.D. 198) Ante-Nicene Fathers vol.3 pg. 687

"Every woman," said he, "praying and prophesying with head uncovered, dishonors her own head." What is "every woman," but woman of every age, of every rank, of every condition? "Every man." As, then, in the masculine sex, under the name of "man" even the "youth" is forbidden to be veiled; so, too, in the feminine, under the name of "woman," even the "virgin" is bidden to be veiled... For indeed it is "on account of the angels" that he said women must be veiled, because on account of "the daughters of men" angels revolted from God. Who then, would contend that "women" alone - that is, such as were already wedded and had lost their virginity - were the objects of angelic concupiscence, unless "virgins" are incapable of excelling in beauty and finding lovers? Tertullian (A.D. 198) Ante-Nicene Fathers vol.3 pg. 688

Why do you denude before God what you cover before men? Will you be more modest in public than in the church? Be veiled, virgin, if virgin you are; for you ought to blush. If you are a virgin, shrink from (the gaze of) many eyes. Let no one wonder at your face; let no one perceive your falsehood. Tertullian (A.D. 198) Ante-Nicene Fathers vol.3 pg. 689

Nay, rather banish quite away from your "free" head all this slavery of ornamentation. In vain do you labor to seem adorned: in vain do you call in the aid of all the most skilful manufacturers of false hair. God bids you "be veiled." I believe (He does so) for fear the heads of some should be seen! Tertullian (A.D. 198) Ante-Nicene Fathers vol.4 pg.22

It behooves our virgins to be veiled from the time that they have passed the turning-point of their age: that this observance is exacted by truth, on which no one can impose prescription - no space of times, no influence of persons, no privilege of regions. Tertullian (A.D. 198) Ante-Nicene Fathers vol.4 pg.27

Throughout Greece, and certain of its barbaric provinces, the majority of Churches keep their virgins covered. There are places, too, beneath this (African) sky, where this practice obtains; lest any ascribe the custom to Greek or barbarian Gentilehood. But I have proposed (as models) those Churches which were founded by apostles or apostolic men. Tertullian (A.D. 198) Ante-Nicene Fathers vol.4 pg.28

"If any," he says, "is contentious, we have not such a custom, nor (has) the Church of God." So, too, did the Corinthians themselves understand him. In fact, at this day the Corinthians do veil their virgins. What the apostles taught, their disciples approve. Tertullian (A.D. 198) Ante-Nicene Fathers vol.4 pg.32-33

But even if it is "on account of the angels" that she is to be veiled, doubtless the age from which the law of the veil will come into operation will be that from which "the daughters of men" were able to invite concupiscence of their persons, and to experience marriage. Tertullian (A.D. 198) Ante-Nicene Fathers vol.4 pg.24

And as they veil their head in presence of heathens, let them at all events in the church conceal their virginity, which they do veil outside the church. They fear strangers: let them stand in awe of the brethren too. Tertullian (A.D. 198) Ante-Nicene Fathers vol.4 pg.35

For some, with their turbans and woolen bands, do not veil their head, but bind it up; protected, indeed, in front, but, where the head properly lies, bare. Others are to a certain extent covered over the region of the brain with linen coifs of small dimensions - I suppose for fear of pressing the head - and not reaching quite to the ears. If they are so weak in their hearing as not to be able to hear through a covering, I pity them. Let them know that the whole head constitutes "the woman." Its limits and boundaries reach as far as the place where the robe begins. The region of the veil is co-extensive with the space covered by the hair when unbound; in order that the necks too may be encircled. For it is they which must be subjected, for the sake of which "power" ought

63

to be "had on the head:" the veil is their yoke. Tertullian (A.D. 198) Ante-Nicene Fathers vol.4 pg.37

Arabia's heathen females will be your judges, who cover not only the head, but the face also, so entirely, that they are content, with one eye free, to enjoy rather half the light than to prostitute the entire face. A female would rather see than be seen. And for this reason a certain Roman queen said that they were most unhappy, in that they could more easily fall in love than be fallen in love with; whereas they are rather happy, in their immunity from that second (and indeed more frequent) infelicity, that females are more apt to be fallen in love with than to fall in love. Tertullian (A.D. 198) Ante-Nicene Fathers vol.4 pg.37

To us the Lord has, even by revelations, measured the space for the veil to extend over. For a certain sister of ours was thus addressed by an angel, beating her neck, as if in applause: "Elegant neck, and deservedly bare! it is well for you to unveil yourself from the head right down to the loins, lest withal this freedom of your neck profit you not!" And, of course, what you have said to one you have said to all. But how severe a chastisement will they likewise deserve, who, amid (the recital of) the Psalms, and at any mention of (the name of) God, continue uncovered; (who) even when about to spend time in prayer itself, with the utmost readiness place a fringe, or a tuft, or any thread whatever, on the crown of their heads, and suppose themselves to be covered? Tertullian (A.D. 198) Ante-Nicene Fathers vol.4 pg.37

AUGUSTINE OF HIPPO:

Chapter 7.—How Man is the Image of God. Whether the Woman is Not Also the Image of God. How the Saying of the Apostle, that the Man is the Image of God, But the Woman is the Glory of the Man, is to Be Understood Figuratively and Mystically. (From On the Holy Trinity; Doctrinal Treatises; Moral Treatises)

9. We ought not therefore so to understand that man is made in the image of the supreme Trinity, that is, in the image of God, as that the same image should be understood to be in three human beings; especially when the apostle says that the man is the image of God, and on that account removes the covering from his head, which he warns the woman to use, speaking thus: "For a man indeed ought not to cover his head, forasmuch as he is the image and glory of God; but the woman is the glory of the man." What then shall we say to this? If the woman fills up the image of the trinity after the measure of her own person, why is the man still

called that image after she has been taken out of his side? Or if even one person of a human being out of three can be called the image of God, as each person also is God in the supreme Trinity itself, why is the woman also not the image of God? For she is instructed for this very reason to cover her head, which he is forbidden to do because he is the image of God.756

10. But we must notice how that which the apostle says, that not the woman but the man is the image of God, is not contrary to that which is written in Genesis, "God created man: in the image of God created He him; male and female created He them: and He blessed them." For this text says that human nature itself, which is complete [only] in both sexes, was made in the image of God; and it does not separate the woman from the image of God which it signifies. For after

Page 159

saying that God made man in the image of God, "He created him," it says, "male and female:" or at any rate, punctuating the words otherwise, "male and female created He them." How then did the apostle tell us that the man is the image of God, and therefore he is forbidden to cover his head; but that the woman is not so, and therefore is commanded to cover hers? Unless, forsooth, according to that which I have said already, when I was treating of the nature of the human mind, that the woman together with her own husband is the image of God, so that that whole substance may be one image; but when she is referred separately to her quality of help-meet, which regards the woman herself alone, then she is not the image of God; but as regards the man alone, he is the image of God as fully and completely as when the woman too is joined with him in one. As we said of the nature of the human mind, that both in the case when as a whole it contemplates the truth it is the image of God; and in the case when anything is divided from it, and diverted in order to the cognition of temporal things; nevertheless on that side on which it beholds and consults truth, here also it is the image of God, but on that side whereby it is directed to the cognition of the lower things, it is not the image of God. And since it is so much the more formed after the image of God, the more it has extended itself to that which is eternal, and is on that account not to be restrained, so as to withhold and refrain itself from thence; therefore the man ought not to cover his head. But because too great a progression towards inferior things is dangerous to that rational cognition that is conversant with things corporeal and temporal;

this ought to have power on its head, which the covering indicates, by which it is signified that it ought to be restrained. For a holy and pious meaning is pleasing to the holy angels.757 For God sees not after the way of time, neither does anything new take place in His vision and knowledge, when anything is done in time and transitorily, after the way in which such things affect the senses, whether the carnal senses of animals and men, or even the heavenly senses of the angels.

11. For that the Apostle Paul, when speaking outwardly of the sex of male and female, figured the mystery of some more hidden truth, may be understood from this, that when he says in another place that she is a widow indeed who is desolate, without children and nephews, and yet that she ought to trust in God, and to continue in prayers night and day,758 he here indicates, that the woman having been brought into the transgression by being deceived, is brought to salvation by child-bearing; and then he has added, "If they continue in faith, and charity, and holiness, with sobriety."759 As if it could possibly hurt a good widow, if either she had not sons, or if those whom she had did not choose to continue in good works. But because those things which are called good works are, as it were, the sons of our life, according to that sense of life in which it answers to the question,

What is a man's life? that is, How does he act in these temporal things? which life the Greeks do not call ζωή but βίος; and because these good works are chiefly performed in the way of offices of mercy, while works of mercy are of no profit, either to Pagans, or to Jews who do not believe in Christ, or to any heretics or schismstics whatsoever in whom faith and charity and sober holiness are not found: what the apostle meant to signify is plain, and in so far figuratively and mystically, because he was speaking of covering the head of the woman, which will remain mere empty words, unless referred to some hidden sacrament.

12. For, as not only most true reason but also the authority of the apostle himself declares, man was not made in the image of God according to the shape of his body, but according to his rational mind. For the thought is a debased and empty one, which holds God to be circumscribed and limited by the lineaments of bodily members. But further, does not the same blessed apostle say, "Be renewed in the spirit of your mind, and put on the new man, which is created after God"; 760 and in another place more clearly, "Putting off the old man," he says, "with his deeds; put on the new man, which is renewed to the knowledge of God after the image of Him that created him"? 761 If, then, we are renewed in

the spirit of our mind, and he is the new man who is renewed to the knowledge of God after the image of Him that created him; no one can doubt, that man was made after the image of Him that created him, not according to the body, nor indiscriminately according to any part of the mind, but according to the rational mind, wherein the knowledge of God can exist. And it is according to this renewal, also, that we are made sons of God by the baptism of Christ; and putting on the new man, certainly put on Christ through faith. Who is there, then,

Page 160

who will hold women to be alien from this fellowship, whereas they are fellow-heirs of grace with us; and whereas in another place the same apostle says, "For ye are all the children of God by faith in Christ Jesus; for as many as have been baptized into Christ have put on Christ: there is neither Jew nor Greek, there is neither bond nor free, there is neither male nor female; for ye are all one in Christ Jesus"? 762 Pray, have faithful women then lost their bodily sex? But because they are there renewed after the image of God, where there is no sex; man is there made after the image of God, where there is no sex, that is, in the spirit of his mind. Why, then, is the man on that account not bound to cover his head, because he is the image and glory of God, while the woman is bound to do so, because she is the glory of the man; as though the woman were not renewed in the spirit of her mind, which spirit is renewed to the knowledge of God after the image of Him who created him? But because she differs from the man in bodily sex, it was possible rightly to represent under her bodily covering that part of the reason which is diverted to the government of temporal things; so that the image of God may remain on that side of the mind of man on which it cleaves to the beholding or the consulting of the eternal reasons of things; and this, it is clear, not men only, but also women have.

Appendix II: Christian Headcovering Quotes and Commentaries

Thomas Goodwin

"All this betokened that angels filled the temple as well as men; and therefore, 1 Cor. xi. 10, (surely it is the meaning of it,) he biddeth women to be modest, to be veiled, to shew subjection, not only because of men, but because of the angels—so the text is here—that are present at their Christian assemblies." (The Works of Thomas Goodwin, Vol. 1, Page 162)

Thomas Adams

"'We are a spectacle of the angels,' 1 Cor. iv. 9: they are observers and witnesses of all of our actions. 'For this cause the woman ought to have power on her head, because of the angels,' 1 Cor. xi. 10. This is not to be understood of offence only given to the ministers of the church; but to signify that a woman throwing off the vail [sic] of modesty, and token of subjection to her husband, doth make even the angels of heaven witnesses of her dissolute contumacy." (The Works of Thomas Adams, Vol. 2, Page 521)

George Swinnock

"First, In honouring [sic] her husband's person. The Persian ladies have the resemblance of a foot worn in the top of their coronets, in token that the top of their glory doth stoop to their husband's feet. The moon, in the sun's absence, takes upon her the government of the heavens; but in his presence she veils herself. The wife, next to her husband, shines in her house, far above all the stars which are fixed there; but God hath appointed that she give place to her husband, and be willing to prefer him. Rebecca, when she approached Isaac, 'took a veil and covered her head,' Gen. xxiv. 56, in token of subjection to her husband; and 'for this cause,' namely, in sign of subjection, 'ought the woman to have power,' that is, a veil, 'over their heads.' 1 Cor. xi. 10, saith the apostle." (The Works of George Swinnock, Volume 1, Page 504)

Thomas Manton

"as the apostle saith, 1 Cor. xl. 10, 'The woman ought to have power on her head, because of the angels.' In the assembly there you meet with angels and devils; angels to observe your garb and carriage, and devils to tempt you; therefore be covered because of the angels. Yet usually women come hither with shameless impudence into the presence of God, men, and angels. This is a practice that neither suits with modesty nor conveniency; nothing can be alleged for it but reasons of pride and wantonness; it feeds your own pride, and provokes lust in others. You would think they were wicked women that should offer others poison to drink; they do that which is worse, lay a snare for the soul; uncover that which should be covered; lest you provoke others of your rank to imitate your vanity, if they should not by the fear of God be guarded from unclean thoughts and filthy desires. Now Christians should be far from allowing sin in themselves, or provoking it in others." (The Works of Thomas Manton, Volume 16, Page 138)

John Calvin

"If the woman uncovers her head, she shakes off subjection—involving contempt of her husband." (Commentary on 1st Corinthians)

"*For it is all one as if she were shaven*. He now maintains from other considerations, that it is unseemly for women to have their heads bare. *Nature itself,* says he, abhors it. To see a woman shaven is a spectacle that is disgusting and monstrous. Hence we infer that the woman *has her hair given for a covering.* Should any one now object, that her hair is enough, as being a natural covering, Paul says that it is *not,* for it is such a covering as requires another thing to be made use of for covering *it.* And hence a conjecture is drawn, with some appearance of probability—that women who had beautiful hair were accustomed to uncover their heads for the purpose of showing off their beauty. It is not, therefore, without good reason that Paul, as a remedy for this vice, sets before them the opposite idea—that they be regarded as remarkable for unseemliness, rather than for what is an incentive to lust." (Commentary on 1st Corinthians)

"*For this cause ought the woman to have power.* From that authority he draws an argument in favor of outward decorum. 'She is subject,' says he, 'let her then wear a token of subjection.' In the term *power,* there is an instance of metonymy, for he means a token by which she declares herself to be under the power of her husband; and it is a covering, whether it be a robe, or a veil, or any other kind of covering." (Commentary on 1st Corinthians)

"When women assume a higher place than becomes them, they gain this by it—that they discover their impudence in the view of the angels of heaven." (Commentary on 1ˢᵗ Corinthians)

Dr. John Gill

(from his Commentary on 1ˢᵗ Corinthians)

1 Corinthians 11:5 But every woman that prayeth or prophesieth,.... Not that a woman was allowed to pray publicly in the congregation, and much less to preach or explain the word, for these things were not permitted them: see 1Co 14:34 but it designs any woman that joins in public worship with the minister in prayer, and attends on the hearing of the word preached, or sings the praises of God with the congregation, as we have seen, the word prophesying signifies,

with her head uncovered. It may seem strange from whom the Corinthian women should take up this custom, since the Jewish women were not allowed to go into the streets, or into any open and public place, unveiled (u). It was a Jewish law, that they should go out no where bare headed (w): yea, it was reckoned scandalous and ignominious to do so. Hence it is said, (x) שגלוי הראש גנאי להם, "that uncovering of the head is a reproach" to the daughters of Israel: and concerning the adulterous woman, it is represented as said by the priest (y), "thou hast separated from the way of the daughters of Israel; for the way or custom of the daughters of Israel is להיות מכוסות ראשיהן, "to have their heads covered"; but thou hast gone "in the ways of the Gentiles", who walk with head bare."

So that their it should seem that these Corinthians followed the examples of the Heathens: but then, though it might be the custom of some nations for women to go abroad bare headed; yet at their solemnities, where and when they were admitted, for they were not everywhere and always, they used to attend with their heads veiled and covered (z). Mr. Mede takes notice indeed of some Heathen priestesses, who used to perform their religious rites and sacrifices with open face, and their hair hanging down, and locks spreading, in imitation of whom these women at Corinth are thought to act. However, whoever behaved in this uncomely manner, whose example soever she followed, the apostle says,

dishonoureth her head; not her husband, who is her head in a figurative sense, and is dishonoured by her not being covered; as if she was not subject to him, or because more beautiful than he, and therefore shows herself; but her natural head, as appears from the reason given:

for that is even all one as if she were shaven; to be without a veil, or some sort of covering on her head, according to the custom of the country, is the same thing as if her head was shaved; and everyone knows how dishonourable and scandalous it is for a woman to have her head shaved; and if this is the same, then it is dishonourable and scandalous to her to be without covering in public worship. And this shows, that the natural head of the man is meant in the preceding verse, since the natural head of the woman is meant in this.

(u) Maimon. Hilch. Ishot, c. 24. sect. 12. (w) T. Bab. Cetubot, fol. 72. 1. (x) R. Sol. Jarchi in Numb. v. 19. (y) Bemidbar Rabba, sect. 9. fol. 193. 2. (z) Alex. ab Alex. Genial. Dier. l. 4. c. 17.

1 Corinthians 11:6 For if the woman be not covered,.... That is, if her head is not covered with some sort of covering, as is the custom of the place where she lives,

let her also be shorn; let her hair be cut

short; let her wear it as men do theirs; and let her see how she will look, and how she will like that, and how she will be looked upon, and liked by others; everybody will laugh at her, and she will be ashamed of herself:

but if it be a shame for a woman to be shorn or shaven: as it is accounted in all civilized nations: the very Heathens (a) speak of it as a thing abominable, and of which there should not be one single dreadful example: then let her be covered; with a veil, or any sort of covering in common use.

(a) Vid. Apul. Metamorph. l. 2. p. 21.

1 Corinthians 11:7 For a man indeed ought not to cover his head,.... The Ethiopic version adds, "whilst he prays"; which is a proper interpretation of the words, though a wrong version; for the apostle's meaning is not, that a man should not have his head covered at any time, but whilst he is in public worship, praying, prophesying, or singing of psalms: the reason is,

forasmuch as he is the image and glory of God. The apostle speaks of man here as in his first creation, in his state of innocence before his fall; but now he has sinned and defaced this image, and come short of this glory; which lay partly in his body being made after the exemplar of the body of Christ, the idea of which God had in his eternal mind, and according to which he shaped the body of Adam: and partly in his soul, in that righteousness and holiness, wisdom and knowledge, and all other excellent gifts in which it was formed. So the Jews (b) say, the understanding is כבוד השם "the glory of God". And it chiefly lay in the power and dominion he had over all the creatures, and even over the woman when made; at least this is principally respected here, in which there is such a shine and representation of the glory and majesty, power and dominion of God; and therefore man ought to worship him with his head uncovered, where this image and glory of God is most illustriously displayed: not but that the woman, is the image and glory of God also, and was made as man, after his image and likeness, with respect to internal qualities, as righteousness, holiness, knowledge, &c. and with regard to her power over the other creatures, though in subjection to man; but yet man was first originally and immediately the image and glory of God, the woman only secondarily and mediately through man. The man is more perfectly and conspicuously the image and glory of God, on account of his more extensive dominion and authority:

but the woman is the glory of the man; being made out of him, and for his help and assistance, and to be a crown of honour and glory to him. The apostle speaks the sense, and in the language of the Jews. The words in Isa 44:13. "After the figure of a man, according to the beauty of a man", are by the Targum

81

rendered, "after the likeness of a man, after the glory of a woman"; and the note of a famous (c) interpreter of theirs upon the last clause is, "this is the woman", שהיא תפארת בעלה "who is the glory of her husband"; but why is she to be covered for this reason, when the man is to be uncovered? it is to be observed, that it is in the presence and worship of God that the one is to be uncovered, and the other covered; the one being the glory of God, and therefore to be uncovered before him; and the other the glory of man, and therefore to be covered before God; and especially, since being first in the transgression, she who is man's glory has been the means of his shame and disgrace. The Jews seem to make this the reason of the difference; they ask (d),

"why does a man go out with his head uncovered, and a woman with her head covered? it is answered, it is like to one that has committed a sin, and he is ashamed of the children of men, therefore she goes וראשה מכוסה, "with her head covered"."

(b) Maimon. in Misn. Chagiga, c. 2. sect 1. 1. (c) R. Sol. Jarchi in Isa. xliv. 13. (d) Bereshit Rabba, sect. 17. fol. 15. 1.

1 Corinthians 11:8 For the man is not of the woman,.... In the present state of things, and according to the ordinary course of generation and propagation of mankind, man is of the woman, though not without the means of man; he is conceived in her, bore by her, and born of her; but the apostle respects the original formation of man, as he was immediately made by God out of the dust of the earth, before the woman was in being, and so not of her:

but the woman of the man; she was made out of his rib, and took both her name and nature from him; God was the author, and man the matter of her being; her original under God, is owing to him; and therefore as he was first in being, he must be superior to her: this serves to prove all that has been as yet said; as that man is the head of the woman, the woman is the glory of man, what he may glory in as being from him; and therefore there should be this difference in their appearance at public worship.

1 Corinthians 11:9 Neither was the man created for the woman,.... To be subservient to her; for she was not in being when he was created; and though it is the proper business of man to provide for, take care of, and defend the woman, as the weaker vessel, yet these were not the original ends of his creation; he was made for God, for his service and glory:

but the woman for the man; to be an help meet for him, who was already created; to be a companion and associate of his, both in religious worship and in civil life; and for the procreation and education of children.

1 Corinthians 11:10 For this cause ought the woman to have power on her head,.... The generality of interpreters, by power, understand the veil, or covering on the woman's head, as a sign of the man's power over her, and her subjection to him; which Dr. Hammond endeavours to confirm, by observing that the Hebrew word רדיד, which signifies a woman's veil, or hood, comes from a root which signifies power and dominion; but in that he is mistaken, for the word is derived not from רדה, to rule, govern, or exercise power and authority, but from רדד, to expand, stretch out, or draw over, as a woman's veil is drawn over her head and face. The Greek word εξουσια more properly signifies the power she had of putting on and off her covering as she pleased, according as times, places, and persons; made it necessary:

because of the angels; various are the senses given of these words, some taking them in a proper, others in a figurative sense: some in a proper sense of angels, and these either good or bad. Tertullian (e) understands them of evil angels, and that a woman should cover her head in time of worship, lest they should lust after her; though much rather the reason should be, lest they should irritate and provoke lust in others: but it is better to understand them of good angels, who attend the assemblies of the saints, and observe the air and behaviour of the worshippers; wherefore women should cover their heads with respect to them, and not give offence to those pure spirits, by an indecent appearance: it is agreeable to the notions of the Jews, that angels attend public prayers, and at the expounding of the word; they often speak (f) of an angel, הממונה על התפלות "that is appointed over prayers"; hence (g) Tertullian seems to have took his notion of an angel of prayer: and of angels being present at expounding of the Scriptures, take the following story (h);

"it happened to Rabban Jochanan ben Zaccai, that he was riding upon an ass, and as he was journeying, R. Eleazar ben Arach was leading an ass after him; he said to him, Rabbi, teach me one chapter in the work of Mercavah (Ezekiel's vision); he replied to him, not so have I taught you, nor in the Mercavah a single man, unless he was a wise man by his own industry; he answered him, Rabbi, give me leave to say one thing before thee, which thou hast taught me; immediately Rabban Jochanan ben Zaccai alighted from his ass and "veiled himself", and sat upon a stone under an olive tree; he said to him, Rabbi, why dost thou alight off from the ass? he replied, is it possible that thou shouldst expound in the work of Mercavah, and the Shekinah be with us, ומלאכי השרת מלוין אותנו, "and the ministering angels join us", and I ride upon an ass?"

And a little after,

"R. Joshua and R. Jose the priest were walking on the road, they said, yea, let us expound in the work of Mercavah; R. Joshua opened and expounded, and that day was the solstice of Tammuz, and the heavens were thickened with clouds, and there appeared the form of a bow in the cloud, "and the ministering angels gathered together", ובאין לשמוע, "and came to hear": as the children of men gather together, and come to see the rejoicings of the bridegroom and bride."

Moreover, this veiling of the woman in public worship because of angels, may be an imitation of the good angels, who when they sung the praises of God, and adored and glorified his perfections, covered their faces and their feet with their wings, Isa 6:1. Many understanding these words in a figurative sense, and in this also they are not agreed; some by angels think young men are meant, who, for their gracefulness and comeliness, are compared to angels; others good men in general, that attend religious worship; others ministers of the word, called angels often in the book of the Revelations; which last seems to be most agreeable of any of these senses; and the women were to cover their heads, that they might not offend either of these, or stir up any impure desires in them; see Ecc 5:6 but as these words follow the account given of the creation of the woman from the man, and for his sake; this may have no reference to her conduct in public worship, but to the power she had of using her covering, or taking it off, or putting it on, at the time of her espousals to a man; which was sometimes done by proxy, or messengers, whom the Jews call שלוחים, "angels" (i); their canon is,

"a man may espouse (a wife) by himself, ובשלוחו, "or by his angel", or messenger; and a woman may be espoused by herself, or by her angel, or messenger:"

wherefore because of these angels, or messengers, that came to espouse her to such, she had power over her head to take off her veil, and show herself, if she thought fit; or to keep it on, as expressing her modesty; or just as she pleased, when she by them was espoused to a man, for whose sake she was made; which sense, after Dr. Lightfoot, many learned men have given into, and seems probable.

(e) De Veland. Virg. c. 7. (f) Shemot Rabba, sect. 21. fol. 106. 2. Zohar. in Gen. fol. 97. 2. (g) De Oratione, c. 15. (h) T. Bab. Chagiga, fol. 14. 2. (i) Misn. Kiddushin, c. 2. sect. 1.

Is the hair alone good enough for a covering?

1 Corinthians 11:15 But if a woman have long hair,.... And wears it, without cutting it, as men do:

it is a glory to her; it is comely and beautiful; it is agreeable to her sex, she looks like herself; it becomes and adorns her:

for her hair is given her for a covering; not instead of a covering for her head, or any other part of her body, so that she needs no other: we read indeed of the daughter of Nicodemus ben Gorion, that she was obliged to make use of her hair for a covering in such a sense (l);

"it happened to R. Jochanan ben Zaccai that he rode upon an ass, and went out of Jerusalem, and his disciples went after him; he saw a young woman gathering barley corns out of the dung of the Arabian cattle; when she saw him, נתעטפה

בשערה, "she covered herself with her hair", and stood before him:"

but this covering was made use of, not of choice, but by force, through her poverty, she having no other; this was not the custom of the nation, nor was the hair given to women for a covering in this sense, nor used by them as such, unless by Eve before the fall; but is rather an indication that they want another covering for their head, it not being so decent that their long hair should be seen. The Jewish women used to esteem it an immodest thing for their hair to be seen, and therefore they took care, as much as possible, to hide it under another covering;

"one woman, whose name was Kimchith, had seven sons, and they all ministered in the high priesthood; the wise men said unto her, what hast thou done, that thou art so worthy? she replied to them, all my days the beams of my house never saw קלעי שערי, "the plaits of my hair" (m);"

that is, they were never seen by any person, even within her house.

(l) T. Bab. Cetubot, fol. 66. 2. (m) T. Bab. Yoma, fol. 47. 1.

Jamieson, Faucett, and Brown Commentary - A.R. Faussett

1 Corinthians 11:15

her hair ... for a covering — Not that she does not need additional covering. Nay, her long hair shows she ought to cover her head as much as possible. The will ought to accord with nature [Bengel]

Albert Barnes

1 Corinthians 11:5

But every woman that prayeth or prophesieth - In the Old Testament prophetesses are not unfrequently mentioned. Thus, Miriam is mentioned Exo 15:20; Deborah Jdg 4:4; Huldah 2Ki 22:14; Noadiah Neh 6:14. So also in the New Testament Anna is mentioned as a prophetess; Luk 2:36. That there were females in the early Christian church who corresponded to those known among the Jews in some measure as endowed with the inspiration of the Holy Spirit, cannot be doubted. What was their precise office, and what was the nature of the public services in which they were engaged, is not however known. That they prayed is clear; and that they publicly expounded the will of God is apparent also; see the note on Act 2:17. As the presumption is, however, that they were inspired, their example is no warrant now for females to take part in the public services of worship, unless they also give evidence that they are under the influence of inspiration, and the more especially as the apostle Paul has expressly forbidden their becoming public teachers; 1Ti 2:12.

If it is now pled, from this example, that women should speak and pray in public, yet it should be just so far only as this example goes, and it should be only when they have the qualifications that the early "prophetesses" had in the Christian church. If there are any such; if any are directly inspired by God, there then will be an evident propriety that they should publicly proclaim the will, and not till then. It may be further observed, however, that the fact that Paul here mentions the custom of women praying or speaking publicly in the church, does not prove that it was right or proper. His immediate object now was not to consider whether the practice was itself right, but to condemn the manner of its performance as a violation of all the proper rules of modesty and of subordination. On another occasion, in this very epistle, he fully condemns the practice in any form, and enjoins silence on the female members of the church in public; 1Co 14:34.

With her head uncovered - That is, with the veil removed which she usually wore. It would seem from this that the women removed their veils, and wore their hair disheveled, when they pretended to be under the influence of divine inspiration. This was the case with the pagan priestesses; and in so doing, the Christian women imitated them. On this account, if on no other, Paul declares the impropriety of this conduct. It was, besides, a custom among ancient females, and one that was strictly enjoined by the traditional laws of the Jews, that a woman should not appear in public unless she were veiled. See this proved by Lightfoot in loco.

Dishonoureth her head - Shows a lack of proper respect to man, to her husband, to her father, to the sex in general. The veil is a token of modesty and of subordination. It is regarded among Jews, and everywhere, as an emblem of her sense of inferiority of rank and station. It is the customary mark of her sex, and that by which she evinces her modesty and sense of subordination. To remove that, is to remove the appropriate mark of such subordination, and is a public act by which she thus shows dishonor to the man. And as it is proper that the grades and ranks of life should be recognized in a suitable manner, so it is improper that, even on pretence of religion, and of being engaged in the service of God, these marks should be laid aside.

For that is even all one as if she were shaven - As if her long hair, which nature teaches her she should wear for a veil (1Co 11:15, margin,) should be cut off. Long hair is, by the custom of the times, and of nearly all countries, a mark of the sex, an ornament of the female, and judged to be beautiful and comely. To remove that is to appear, in this respect, like the other sex, and to lay aside the badge of her own. This, says Paul, all would judge to be improper. You yourselves would not allow it. And yet to lay aside the veil - the appropriate badge of the sex, and of her sense of subordination - would be an act of the same kind. It would indicate the same feeling, the same forgetfulness of the proper sense of subordination; and if that is laid aside, all the usual indications of modesty and subordination might be removed also. Not even under religious pretences, therefore, are the usual marks of sex, and of propriety of place and rank, to be laid aside. Due respect is to be shown, in dress, and speech, and deportment, to those whom God has placed above us; and neither in language, in attire nor in habit are we to depart from what all judge to he proprieties of life, or from what God has judged and ordained to be the proper indications of the regular gradations in society.

1 Corinthians 11:6

For if the woman be not covered - If her head be not covered with a veil.

Let her also be shorn - Let her long hair be cut off. Let her lay aside all the usual and proper indications of her sex and rank in life. If it is done in one respect, it may with the same propriety be done in all.

But if it be a shame ... - If custom, nature, and habit; if the common and usual feelings and views among people would pronounce this to be a shame, the other would be pronounced to be a shame also by the same custom and common sense of people.

Let her be covered - With a veil. Let her wear the customary attire indicative of modesty and a sense of subordination. Let her not lay this aside even on any pretence of religion.

1 Corinthians 11:7

For a man indeed ought not to cover his head - That is, with a veil; or in public worship; when he approaches God, or when in His name he addresses his fellow man. It is not fit and proper that he should be covered. The reason why it is not proper, the apostle immediately states.

Forasmuch as he is the image and glory of God - The phrase "the image of God" refers to the fact that man was made in the likeness of his Maker Gen 1:27; and proves that, though fallen, there is a sense in which he is still the image of God. It is not because man is truly or pure, and thus resembles his Creator; but it evidently is because he was invested by his Maker with authority and dominion; he was superior to all other creatures; Gen 1:28. This is still retained; and this the apostle evidently refers to in the passage before us, and this he says should be recognized and regarded. If he wore a veil or turban, it would be a mark of servitude or inferiority. It was therefore improper that he should appear in this manner; but he should he so clad as not to obscure or hide the great truth that he was the direct representative of God on the earth, and had a superiority to all other creatures.

And glory of God - The word "glory" in the classic writers means:

(1) Opinion, sentiment, etc.;

(2) fame, reputation.

Here it means, as it often does, splendor, brightness, or that which stands forth to "represent" God, or by which the glory of God is known. Man was created first; he had dominion given him; by him, therefore, the divine authority and wisdom first shone forth; and this fact should be recognized in the due subordination of rank, and even in the apparel and attire which shall be worn. The impression of his rank and superiority should be everywhere retained.

But the woman is the glory of the man - The honor, the ornament, etc. She was made for him; she was made after he was; she was taken from him, and was "bone of his bone, and flesh of his flesh." All her comeliness, loveliness, and purity are therefore an expression of his honor and dignity, since all that comeliness and loveliness were made of him and for him. This, therefore, ought to be acknowledged by a suitable manner of attire; and in his presence this sense of her inferiority of rank and subordination should be acknowledged by the customary use of the veil. She should appear with the symbol of modesty and subjection, which are implied by the head being covered This sense is distinctly expressed in the following verse.

1 Corinthians 11:8

For the man is not of the woman - The man was not formed from the woman.

But the woman of the man - From his side; Gen_2:18, Gen_2:22-23.

1 Corinthians 11:9

Neither was the man created for the woman ... - This is a simple statement of what is expressed in Genesis. The woman was made for the comfort and happiness of the man. Not to be a slave, but a help-meet; not to be the minister of his pleasures, but to be his aid and comforter in life; not to be regarded as of inferior nature and rank, but to be his friend, to divide his sorrows, and to multiply and extend his joys; yet still to be in a station subordinate to him. He is to be the head: the ruler; the presider in the family circle; and she was created to aid him in his duties, to comfort him in his afflictions, to partake with him of his pleasures. Her rank is therefore honorable, though it is subordinate. It is, in some respects, the more honorable because it is subordinate and as her happiness is dependent on him, she has the higher claim to his protection and his tender care. The whole of Paul's idea here is, that her situation and rank as subordinate should be recognized by her at all times, and that in his presence it was proper that she should wear the usual symbol of modesty and subordination, the veil.

1 Corinthians 11:10

For this cause ... - There is scarcely any passage in the Scriptures which has more exercised the ingenuity of commentators than this verse. The various attempts which have been made to explain it may be seen in Pool, Rosenmuller, Bloomfield, etc. After all the explanations which have been given of it, I confess, I do not understand it. It is not difficult to see what the connection requires us to suppose in the explanation. The obvious interpretation would be, that a woman should have a veil on her head because of the angels who were supposed to be present, observing them in their public worship; and it is generally agreed that the word "power" (ἐξουσίαν exousian) denotes a veil, or a covering for the head. But the word power does not occur in this sense in any classic writer. Bretschneider understands it of a veil, as being a defense or guard to the face, lest it should be seen by others. Some have supposed that it was the name of a female ornament that was worn on the head, formed of braids of hair set with jewels. Most commentators agree that it means a "veil," though some think (see Bloomfield) that it is called power to denote the veil which was worn by married women, which indicated the superiority of the married woman to the maiden. But it is sufficient to say in reply to this, that the apostle is not referring to married women in contradistinction from those who are unmarried, but is showing that all women who prophecy or pray in public should be veiled. There can, perhaps, be no doubt that the word "power" has reference to a veil, or to a covering for the head; but why it is called power I confess I do not understand; and most of the comments on the word are, in my view, egregious trifling.

Because of the angels - Some have explained this of good angels, who were supposed to be present in their assemblies (see Doddridge); others refer it to evil angels; and others to messengers or spies who, it has been supposed, were present in their public assemblies, and who would report greatly to the disadvantage of the Christian assemblies if the women were seen to be unveiled. I do not know what it means; and I regard it as one of the very few passages in the Bible whose meaning as yet is wholly inexplicable. The most natural interpretation seems to me to be this: "A woman in the public assemblies, and in speaking in the presence of people, should wear a veil - the usual symbol of modesty and subordination - because the angels of God are witnesses of your public worship Heb 1:13, and because they know and appreciate the propriety of subordination and order in public assemblies."

According to this, it would mean that the simple reason would be that the angels were witnesses of their worship; and that they were the friends of propriety, due subordination, and order; and that they ought to observe these in all assemblies convened for the worship of God - I do not know that this sense has been proposed by any commentator; but it is one which strikes me as the most obvious and natural, and consistent with the context. The following remarks respecting the ladies of Persia may throw some light on this subject - "The head-dress of the women is simple; their hair is drawn behind the head, and divided into several tresses; the beauty of this head-dress consists in the thickness and length of these tresses, which should fall even down to the heels, in default of which, they lengthen them with tresses of silk. The ends of these tresses they decorate with pearls and jewels, or ornaments of gold or silver. The head is covered, "under" the veil or kerchief "(course chef)," only by the end of a small "bandeau," shaped into a triangle; this "bandeau," which is of various colors, is thin and light.

The "bandalette" is embroidered by the needle, or covered with jewelry, according to the quality of the wearer. This is, in, my opinion, the ancient "tiara," or "diadem," of the queens of Persia. Only married women wear it; and it is the mark by which it is known that they are under subjection "(oc'est la la marque a laquelle on reconnoit qu' elles sont sous puissance o - power)." The girls have little "caps," instead of this kerchief or tiara; they wear no veil at home, but let two tresses of their hair fall under their cheeks. The caps of girls of superior rank are tied with a row of pearls. Girls are not shut up in Persia till they attain the age of six or seven years; before that age they go out of the seraglio, sometimes with their father, so that they may then be seen. I have seen some wonderfully pretty girls. They show the neck and bosom; and more beautiful cannot be seen" - Chardin. "The wearing of a veil by a married woman was a token of her being under power. The Hebrew name of the veil signifies dependence. Great importance was attached to this part of the dress in the East. All the women of Persia are pleasantly apparelled. When they are abroad in the streets, all, both rich and poor, are covered with a great veil, or sheet of very fine white cloth, of which one half, like a forehead cloth, comes down to the eyes, and, going over the head, reaches down to the heels; and the other half muffles up the face below the eyes, and being fastened with a pin to the left side of the head, falls down to their very shoes, even covering their hands, with which they hold that cloth by the two sides, so that, except the eyes, they are covered all over with it. Within doors they have their faces and breasts uncovered; but the Armenian women in their houses have always one half of their faces covered with a cloth, that goes athwart their noses, and hangs over their chin and breasts, except the maids of that nation, who, within doors, cover only the chin until they are married" - Thevenot.

The Geneva Bible

1 Corinthians 11:5 (4) But every woman that prayeth or prophesieth with [her] head uncovered dishonoureth her head: (5) for that is even all one as if she were shaven.

(4) And in like manner he concludes that women who show themselves in public and ecclesiastical assemblies without the sign and token of their subjection, that is to say, uncovered, shame themselves. (5) The first argument taken from the common sense of man, for so much as nature teaches women that it is dishonest for them to go abroad bareheaded, seeing that they have given to them thick and long hair which they do so diligently trim and deck, that they can in no way abide to have it shaved.

Matthew Henry

1 Corinthians 11:1-16

Paul, having answered the cases put to him, proceeds in this chapter to the redress of grievances. The first verse of the chapter is put, by those who divided the epistle into chapters, as a preface to the rest of the epistle, but seems to have been a more proper close to the last, in which he had enforced the cautions he had given against the abuse of liberty, by his own example: *Be ye followers of me, as I also am of Christ* (1Co 11:1), fitly closes his argument; and the way of speaking in the next verse looks like a transition to another. But, whether it more properly belong to this or the last chapter, it is plain from it that Paul not only preached such doctrine as they ought to believe, but led such a life as they ought to imitate. "Be ye followers of me," that is, "Be imitators of me; live as you see me live." Note, Ministers are likely to preach most to the purpose when they can press their hearers to follow their example. Yet would not Paul be followed blindly neither. He encourages neither implicit faith nor obedience. He would be followed himself no further than he followed Christ. Christ's pattern is a copy without a blot; so is no man's else. Note, We should follow no leader further than he follows Christ. Apostles should be left by us when they deviate from the example of their Master. He passes next to reprehend and reform an indecency among them, of which the women were more especially guilty, concerning which observe,

I. How he prefaces it. He begins with a commendation of what was praiseworthy in them (1Co 11:2): *I praise you, that you remember me in all things, and keep the ordinances as I delivered them to you.* Many of them, it is probable, did this in the strictest sense of the expression: and he takes occasion thence to address the body of the church under this good character; and the body might, in the main, have continued to observe the ordinances and institutions of Christ, though in some things they deviated fRom. and corrupted, them. Note, When we reprove what is amiss in any, it is very prudent and fit to commend what is good in them; it will show that the reproof is not from ill-will, and a humour of censuring and finding fault; and it will therefore procure the more regard to it.

II. How he lays the foundation for his reprehension by asserting the superiority of the man over the woman: *I would have you know that the head of every man is Christ, and the head of the woman is the man, and the head of Christ is God.* Christ, in his mediatorial character and glorified humanity, is at the head of mankind. He is not only first of the kind, but Lord and Sovereign. He has a name above

104

every name: though in this high office and authority he has a superior, God being his head. And as God is the head of Christ, and Christ the head of the whole human kind, so the man is the head of the two sexes: not indeed with such dominion as Christ has over the kind or God has over the man Christ Jesus; but a superiority and headship he has, and the woman should be in subjection and not assume or usurp the man's place. This is the situation in which God has placed her; and for that reason she should have a mind suited to her rank, and not do any thing that looks like an affectation of changing places. Something like this the women of the church of Corinth seem to have been guilty of, who were under inspiration, and prayed and prophesied even in their assemblies, 1Co 11:5. It is indeed an apostolical canon, that the women *should keep silence in the churches* (1Co 14:34; 1Ti 2:12), which some understand without limitation, as if a woman under inspiration also must keep silence, which seems very well to agree with the connection of the apostle's discourse, ch. 14. Others with a limitation: though a woman might not from her own abilities pretend to teach, or so much as question and debate any thing in the church yet when under inspiration the case was altered, she had liberty to speak. Or, though she might not preach even by inspiration (because teaching is the business of a superior), yet she might pray or utter hymns by inspiration, even in the public assembly. She did not show any affectation of superiority over the man by such acts of public worship. It is plain the apostle does not in this place prohibit the thing, but reprehend the manner of doing it. And yet he might utterly disallow the thing and lay an unlimited restraint on the woman in another part of the epistle. These things are not contradictory. It is to his present purpose to reprehend the manner wherein the women prayed and prophesied in the church, without determining in this place whether they did well or ill in praying or prophesying. Note, The manner of doing a thing enters into the morality of it. We must not only be concerned to do good, but that the good we do be well done.

III. The thing he reprehends is the woman's praying or prophesying uncovered, or the man's doing either covered, 1Co 11:4, 1Co 11:5. To understand this, it must be observed that it was a signification either of shame or subjection for persons to be veiled, or covered, in the eastern countries, contrary to the custom of ours, where the being bare-headed betokens subjection, and being covered superiority and dominion. And this will help us the better to understand,

IV. The reasons on which he grounds his reprehension. 1. *The man that prays or prophesies with his head covered dishonoureth his head,* namely, Christ, the head of every man (1Co 11:3), by appearing in a habit unsuitable to the rank in which God has placed him. Note, We should, even in our dress and habits, avoid every thing that may dishonour Christ. *The woman,* on the other hand, *who prays or prophesies with her head uncovered dishonoureth her head,* namely, the man, 1Co 11:3. She appears in the dress of her superior, and throws off the token of her subjection. She might, with equal decency, cut her hair short, or cut it close, which was the custom of the man in that age. This would be in a manner to declare that she was desirous of changing sexes, a manifest affectation of that superiority which God had conferred on the other sex. And this was probably the fault of these prophetesses in the church of Corinth. It was doing a thing which, in that age of the world, betokened superiority, and therefore a tacit claim of what did not belong to them but the other sex. Note, The sexes should not affect to change places. The order in which divine wisdom has placed persons and things is best and fittest: to endeavour to amend it is to destroy all order, and introduce confusion. The woman should keep to the rank God has chosen for her, and not dishonour her head; for this, in the result, is to dishonour God. If she was made out of the man, and for the man, and made to be the glory of the man, she should do nothing, especially in public, that looks like a wish of having this order inverted. 2. Another reason against this conduct is that *the man is the image and glory of God,* the representative of that glorious dominion and headship which God has over the world. It is the man who is set at the head of this lower creation, and therein he bears the resemblance of God. The woman, on the other hand, *is the glory of the man* (1Co 11:7): she is his representative. Not but she has dominion over the inferior creatures, as she is a partaker of human nature, and so far is God's representative too, but it is at second-hand. She is the image of God, inasmuch as she is the image of the man: *For the man was not made out of the woman, but the woman out of the man,* 1Co 11:8. The man was first made, and made head of the creation here below, and therein the image of the divine dominion; and the woman was made out of the man, and shone with a reflection of his glory, being made superior to the other creatures here below, but in subjection to her husband, and deriving that honour from him out of whom she was made. 3. *The woman was made for the man,* to be his help-meet, *and not the man for the woman.* She was naturally, therefore, made subject to him, because made for him, for his use, and help, and comfort. And she who was intended to be always in subjection to the man should do nothing, in Christian assemblies, that looks like an affectation of equality. 4. *She ought to have power on her head, because of the angels.* Power, that is, a veil, the token, not of her having the power or superiority, but being under the power of her husband, subjected to him, and inferior to the other sex. Rebekah, when she met Isaac, and was delivering herself into his possession, put on her veil, in token of her subjection, Gen 24:65. Thus would the apostle have the women appear In Christian assemblies, even though they spoke there by inspiration, *because of the angels,* that is, say some, because of the evil angels. The woman *was first in the transgression, being deceived by the devil* (1Ti 2:14), which increased her subjection to man, Gen 3:16. Now, believe evil angels will be sure to mix in all Christian assemblies, therefore should women wear the token of their shamefacedness and subjection, which in that age and country, was a veil. Others say because of the good angels. Jews and Christians have had an opinion that these ministering spirits are many of them present in their assemblies. Their presence should restrain Christians from all indecencies in the worship of God. Note, We should learn from all to behave in the public assemblies of divine worship so as to express a reverence for God, and a content and satisfaction with that rank in which he has placed us.

V. He thinks fit to guard his argument with a caution lest the inference be carried too far (1Co 11:11, 1Co 11:12): *Nevertheless, neither is the man without the woman, nor the woman without the man in the Lord.* They were made for one another. *It is not good for him to be alone* (Gen 2:18), and therefore was a woman made, and made for the man; and the man was intended to be a comfort, and help, and defence, to the woman, though not so directly and immediately made for her. They were made to be a mutual comfort and blessing, not one a slave and the other a tyrant. *Both were to be one flesh* (Gen 2:24), and this for the propagation of a race of mankind. They are reciprocal instruments of each other's production. As the woman was first formed out of the man, the man is ever since propagated by the woman (1Co 11:12), all by the divine wisdom and power of the First Cause so ordaining it. The authority and subjection should be no greater than are suitable to two in such near relation and close union to each other. Note, As it is the will of God that the woman know her place, so it is his will also that the man abuse not his power.

VI. He enforces his argument from the natural covering provided for the woman (1Co_11:13-15): "*Judge in yourselves* - consult your own reason, hearken to what nature suggests - *is it comely for a woman to pray to God uncovered?* Should there not be a distinction kept up between the sexes in wearing their hair, since nature has made one? Is it not a distinction which nature has kept up among all civilized nations? The woman's hair is a natural covering; to wear it long is a glory to her; but for a man to have long hair, or cherish it, is a token of softness and effeminacy." Note, It should be our concern, especially in Christian and religious assemblies, to make no breach upon the rules of natural decency.

VII. He sums up all by referring those who were contentious to the usages and customs of the churches, 1Co_11:16. Custom is in a great measure the rule of decency. And the common practice of the churches is what would have them govern themselves by. He does not silence the contentious by mere authority, but lets them know that they would appear to the world as very odd and singular in their humour if they would quarrel for a custom to which all the churches of Christ were at that time utter strangers, or against a custom in which they all concurred, and that upon the ground of natural decency. It was the common usage of the churches for women to appear in public assemblies, and join in public worship, veiled; and it was manifestly decent that they should do so. Those must be very contentious indeed who would quarrel with this, or lay it aside.

How You Can Help

Bringing a book or tract of any size to print can be an enormous undertaking, especially for an independent author. I have relied on friends and neighbors to help me get this material out to the world, because for any independently published work to reach a wider audience, the author must ask for the help of those who also believe in the work and message.

On behalf of all independent authors I'd like to ask you to help as well. When you come across an independently published book, tract, story, or other material that you feel has value, would you do what you can to share your find? Sometimes just letting others within your circle know that a work exists can multiply the efforts of the author and those who have helped give birth to the work.

Please tell your friends about it, mention it on Facebook, or find other ways to spread the word about it. Independent authors will only rarely see their work widely received and accepted, and most indie authors do not have the money for large advertising campaigns. Word of mouth is our best advertising.

One of the greatest and most beneficial things you can do to help an independent work of value is to take just a few moments to review that work on

Amazon. Good ratings do help and so does a good review. When people take time to share and review a work they have found to be of value, others who might be benefited from or who might enjoy a work can get a better idea of whether or not that work is worth their time.

Would you take the time to review this work on Amazon?

Again, I thank you so much for your help.

Michael Bunker

Other Books in this series...

The Beard, by Michael Bunker

Available Now

ISBN: 9781481254564

A Must Read Non-Fiction book by Michael Bunker:

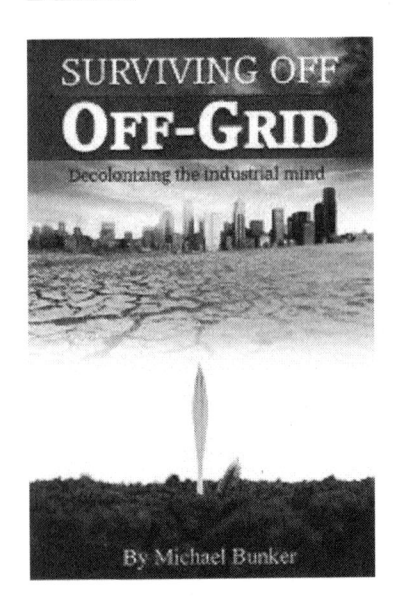

Surviving Off Off-Grid:
Decolonizing the Industrial Mind

ISBN: 0615447902

A Review of *Surviving Off Off-Grid* by Herrick Kimball of The Deliberate Agrarian blog:

Speaking of books, I have read a prepublication copy of Michael Bunker's soon-to-be-released new book, *Surviving Off Off-Grid: Decolonizing The Industrial Mind*. Fact is, I've read most of the book twice, and underlined numerous passages. Yes, it's that good.

I noticed that another blogger has reviewed this book and described it as "profound." I thought that was an interesting conclusion because it was exactly the descriptive word that came to my mind as I was reading it. My dictionary defines profound as "penetrating beyond what is superficial or obvious," and that certainly does sum it up.

The way it looks to me, there are three categories of people who will appreciate what this book has to say, and who will benefit from it. First would be anyone who is thinking of living off grid. Second would be anyone who has an interest in surviving economic and civilizational collapse. Third would be those people who have an interest in Biblical agrarianism and cultural separation. I suppose I would fall into all three categories, but my primary interest is Biblical agrarianism, so I'm going to focus on that in this review. I should mention that Michael makes the point that readers of his book need not be Christians to benefit from the practical outlook and ideas in the book. That is true.

In the foreword of his book Michael writes:

"it is our intention to offer a philosophy that, whatever may be said of it, stands Contra Mundum (against the world), and against the prevailing foundational philosophy of industrial consumerism, thoughtless consumption, and the dependence on systems that are contrary to our own best interests."

Look in the top right corner of this page and you will see that I say this here blog of mine is a "rich resource of contra-industrial thought..." It so happens that Michael Bunker and I are on the same page when it comes to seeing wicked industrialism for what it really is.

Our disdain for industrialism comes from our scriptural understandings. We believe the Bible calls Christians to separate not only from common forms of worldly immorality, but also the more subtle immorality of worldly dependencies too.

Of course, those who hold to Christian-agrarian beliefs are not just a minority, but a *minuscule* minority. That fact is probably sufficient to discount the legitimacy of Christian-agrarianism in the minds of the majority. But God has always done his greatest works through a humble minority of faithful followers.

Nevertheless, I must say that I still find it amazing that mainstream evangelical Christianity, with its continual end-times observations and prognostications, doesn't seem to realize (or care) that its followers support, and draw their sustenance from, a one-world, industrial-beast system, right here and now. They cleave to the system, and they love the system. Hello?

So it is that precious few people who consider themselves to be Christians see the corporate-industrial system as something to separate from. Their minds have been "colonized" along with everyone else's. After all, no mainline denomination or popular televangelist is espousing separation from the industrial system. It's not even on their radar screens.

Where Michael and I differ in our Biblical agrarian apologetics is in the ability to formulate a cogent and comprehensive contra-industrial argument. I only scratch the surface in my writings, while Michael Bunker digs deep. His new book makes this abundantly clear.

The other difference is the degree to which each of us has separated from industrial grid dependencies. I feel like I am physically positioned to live off-grid if/when the system crashes—not for a week or a month, but for the rest of my life. That isn't to say I'm stocked with a good supply of batteries and fuel and survival food, because I'm not. I'm stocked with tools and hands-on experience for living very simply, and providing for my basic life needs apart from the industrial system. To this end, little by slow, I continue to make more progress all the time. I also believe that, by the grace of God, I have the spiritual resources to deal with the transition. But Michael and his family are already living off grid, or beyond off-grid, or, as the book says *Off Off-Grid*. So he is well qualified to write this book.

Fact is, he is uniquely qualified—no one else I know of is saying, or putting into words, the things Michael Bunker is saying in this book. It is an incredibly thought provoking read. And, as far as I'm concerned, what he is saying is not only contra mundum, it's right on.

You should know that, regardless of the title, this book is not so much about surviving the inevitable crash of the industrial nations, it's about deliberately choosing to live apart from the industrial grid for philosophical and religious reasons, regardless of whether it crashes or not. The subtitle of the book, "Decolonizing the Industrial Mind" is really more to the point.

I was struck by a biblical reference in the book under the heading of "Old Paths." Much of Michael's book is about thinking in pre-grid ways and dealing with problems creatively. Michael mentions Jeremiah 6:16. That verse and the idea of returning to the "old paths' just happens to figure prominently in the book I am currently working on. Coincidence? Hmmm. Here's what Michael writes:

Looking towards the old paths is not a melancholy dream, or some fantastical wish for a mythical bygone paradise. We don't look to the past as if it was the perfect, idyllic, pastoral utopia. We know it wasn't perfect. We look to the past for a few great reasons: Because the Bible tells us to (Jer. 6:16); because there is wisdom and reason in learning these old and valued skills; and because the way the world has chosen, though it seems to be right for a time, has wrought nothing but damage, destruction, intellectual and spiritual entropy, and mental colonization. The product of the modern way of doing things is spiritual emptiness and sadness, is fraught with disappointment and unrealized expectations, and creates a crazed urge to fill the void with consumption and "stuff."

Surviving Off Off-Grid touches on many different specific subjects: debt slavery, acquiring land, off-grid heat, light & refrigeration, water, food, housing, and much more.

If you are a thinking person, if you don't mind having your ingrained industrial-world suppositions challenged, if you are desiring to live a more genuine and satisfying life, if you are a person concerned about the coming collapse of western civilization, if you are looking for some rock-solid nuggets of real wisdom in the midst of a world that is blinded by fool's gold, this book is for you.

In the final analysis, I'm not sure what category *Surviving Off Off-Grid* would fall into. It is full of philosophy, psychology, sociology, religion (Christianity), history and (to a small degree) there is some general how-to. Perhaps it would best fit in the just-plain-down-to-earth-good-sense category. Contra mundum, of course.

If you were benefited by this book you can visit Michael Bunker on Facebook and Twitter.

Michael Bunker on Facebook:
http://facebook.com/michaelbunker

Michael's Twitter:
http://twitter.com/mbunker (@mbunker)

Other Books by Michael Bunker

Surviving Off Off-Grid, by Michael Bunker (2011).
ISBN 9780615447902

Modern Religious Idols, by Michael Bunker (2011).
ISBN 9780615498317

Swarms of Locusts: The Jesuit Attack on the Faith, by Michael Bunker (2002).
ISBN 0595252974

The Last Pilgrims, by Michael Bunker (2012).
ISBN 978-0578088891

The Beard, by Michael Bunker (2012).
ISBN 9781481254564

WICK, by Michael Bunker (2013).
ISBN 9781481858342

Michael Bunker constrains most of his communication to *"snail mail"* (traditional post). Please write him a letter if you have questions, comments, or suggestions. Michael does keep a very small, very intimate email alert list. To receive Michael Bunker's e-mail alerts, which are rare but do include notifications when new sermons or podcasts are posted, and updates on Michael's ministry, ministry trips, etc., please send an e-mail to:

mbunker@michaelbunker.com

To listen to the Michael Bunker Radio Show please go to:

www.blogtalkradio.com/michaelbunker.

You can subscribe to Michael's show on iTunes.com

M. Bunker

1251 CR 132

Santa Anna, Texas 76878